THE
WARNER BROS. STUDIOS
COMMISSARY COOKBOOK

A WARNER BROS. STUDIOS PUBLICATION

Copyright 2016 © Warner Bros. Studios

A Warner Bros. Studios Book | Rare Bird Books
453 South Spring Street, Suite 302
Los Angeles, CA 90013
rarebirdbooks.com

FIRST HARDCOVER EDITION

Set in Minion
Printed in Canada

Food photography by Anjali Pinto, supplemental photography by Alice Marsh-Elmer.

10 9 8 7 6 5 4 3 2 1

Publisher's Cataloging-in-Publication data

Names: Warner Bros.
Title: The Warner Bros. Studios Commissary Cookbook.
Description: A Warner Bros. Studios Book | First Hardcover Edition | New York [New York] ; Los Angeles [California] : Rare Bird Books, 2016. | Includes index.
Identifiers: ISBN 978-1-942600-80-0.
Subjects: LCSH Warner Bros. Studios Commissary. | Cooking, American. | Cookbooks. | BISAC COOKING / Individual Chefs & Restaurants.
Classification: LCC TX945.5 .W37 W37 2016| DDC 641.50979493—dc23

THE
WARNER BROS. STUDIOS
COMMISSARY COOKBOOK

WARNER BROS. STUDIOS | RARE BIRD BOOKS

CONTENTS

NOTES FROM THE CHEFS

The Warner Bros. Studios commissary dining room and adjacent employee cafeteria were originally operated as part of the First National Pictures Studios, acquired by Warner Bros. Studios in 1928. From that point forward, and still to the present day, our highly skilled cooks work hard to satisfy the discerning tastes of our entire studio family.

The recipes and plate presentations in this cookbook are representative of what has been featured in the commissary. We have taken care to include those dishes which we believe will be most enjoyed by your family and friends.

GABRIEL MORALES

MAURIZIO BINOTTO

HORS D'OUVRES

Imported Russian Caviar 75   Pate de Foie Gras 60   Anchovies 50
Assorted Canapes 1.25   Imported Natural Gooseliver

COCKTAILS

Oyster or Shrimp Cocktail 50   Fruit Cocktail 30
Lobster or Crabmeat 50   Grapefruit Supreme 45

RELISHES

Hearts of Celery 20   Ripe Olives 20   Avocado Half 60   Stuffed Celery 35
Dill Pickles 15   Sweet Pickles 15   Sweet Relish 15

OYSTERS—SEA FOOD
(In Season)

Oysters (½ dozen), Fried 60, Raw 50   Milk Stew 50   Cream Stew 65
Broiled Lobster (half) 85   Cold Boiled Lobster (half) 85
Shrimp, Lobster, Crab a la Newberg 75   Oyster Pancake 75

STEAKS, CHOPS, CHICKEN, Etc.

Tenderloin 90   New York Cut Sirloin 80   Steak Minute 75   T-Bone Steak 75
French Lamb Chops (2) 60   Veal Cutlet 50; Breaded 60   Pork Chops (2) 50
Broiled Ham or Bacon 40   Holstein Schnitzel 75   Ham Steak 60
Tartar Steak 60   Chicken a la King 75   Top Sirloin 65   Club Steak 60
Pounded Steak 50   Hamburger 45   Little Pig Sausage 45
½ Broiled Chicken 75   Special Steak Sandwich 75

SAUCES

Tomato 15   Mushroom 35   Bordelaise 20   Spanish 15   Chili Sauce 10
Smothered Onions 15   French Fried Onions 35   Country Gravy 15

EGGS—OMELETTES
(Two Eggs to the Order; Each Additional Egg 10)

Cinnamon Toast 25   French Toast 35
Eggs, Boiled, Fried or Scrambled 25   Shirred 30   Poached on Toast 30
Eggs Vienna 50   Omelette, Plain 25   Omelette with Tomatoes 40
Omelette with Jelly 40   Omelette with Ham or Bacon 45   French Pancake 75
German Pancake 75   Omelette with Parsley 40
Spanish Omelette 45   Oyster Omelette 60   Chicken Liver Omelette 65
Omelette with Cheese 50   Omelette with Asparagus Tips 55
Ham or Bacon and Eggs 40   Side Order Bacon 15   Side Order Ham 20
Ham and Corn Omelette 50   Onion Omelette 40   Omelette Country Style 55

POTATOES—VEGETABLES

French Fried 15   Hashed Brown 15   American Fried 15   Lyonnaise 20
Cottage Fried 25   Julienne 20   Au Gratin 25   Long Branch 20
Sugar Corn 15   Green Peas 15   String Beans 15   Shoe Strings 25
Stewed Tomatoes 15   California Asparagus, Drawn Butter 30
Spinach 15; with Egg 25   Baby Limas 20   O'Brien 25

Fresh Vegetables 5c Extra

Original cafe menu, circa 1928.

COLD MEATS
(With Potato Salad)

Boiled Ham 50   Baked Spiced Ham 60   Sliced Chicken, Fruit Salad 75
Assorted Cold Meats 50   Sardines, Imported 50; Imported French 75
Sliced Turkey 85   Baked Ham and Tomatoes 65
Assorted Cold Meats with Chicken 70

SALADS
(With French Dressing)

Head Lettuce 20   Sliced Tomatoes 25   Combination 35; half 20
Lettuce and Tomato 25   Lettuce and Egg 30
Pineapple and Cottage Cheese 35; half 20   Waldorf 35   Asparagus Tips 35
Chicken 50   Lobster 50   Crabmeat 50   Shrimp 50   Tuna 40
Potato 15   Tomato Stuffed with Chicken Salad 50   Cold Slaw 15
Pineapple and Cream Cheese 45   Fruit Salad 30; with Whipped Cream 40
Roquefort Cheese Dressing 25   Russian 25   Mayonnaise 15

SANDWICHES

First National Special (Ham, Cheese, Chicken on Toast) 40
Manager Special (Peanut Butter, Baked Ham, Chicken on Toast) 35
Chef's Special (Ham, Jam, Chicken) 35
Ham, Cheese, Jelly, 3-Deckers on Toast 30   Bacon and Lettuce on Toast 30
Hamburger 15   Boiled Ham 10   Fried Ham 15   Baked Ham 15
Ham and Egg 25   Fried Egg 15   Denver 25   Tuna Salad 15
Deviled Egg 15   Tuna 25   Tongue 20   Chicken 35   Club House 50
Chicken Salad 25   Sardine 20   American Cheese 10   Pimiento Cheese 15
Swiss Cheese, Domestic 10; Imported 25   Toasted Cheese 25
Lettuce and Tomato 15   Lettuce, Mayonnaise 15   Peanut Butter 10
Steak Sandwich on Toast 50   Minced Olive on Toast 20   Roast Beef, Cold 15
Liverwurst 20   Cream Cheese 25   Prime Rib 35   Corned Beef 15   Salami 20

DESSERTS

Assorted Pies 10   Layer Cake 15   Pound Cake 10   Vanilla Ice Cream 10
Chocolate Ice Cream 10   Sherbet 10   Chocolate Nut Sundae 20
Parfait 25   Baked Apple 15; with Cream 20   Sliced Pineapple 15
Bartlett Pears 15   Lemon Cling Peaches 15   Orange Marmalade 20
Strawberry Preserves 20   Preserved Figs 20   Royal Ann Cherries 20
Apricots 20   Cheese Cake 15   Chocolate Eclair 15

CHEESE

American 15   Swiss Domestic 15; Imported 25   Roquefort 25   Cottage 20
Limburger 20   Camembert 25   Cream Cheese 20   Gruyere 20

DRINKS

Coffee 10; with Meal 5; Pot 15   Tea, Pot 10   Milk 10   Buttermilk 10
Iced Tea 10   Hot Chocolate 10; with Whipped Cream 15   Iced Coffee 10
Cocoa, Cup 10   Glass Half and Half 25   Postum 10
Orange Juice 10-20   Eastside 15   Canada Dry Ginger Ale 30
Malted Milk; with Egg 25   White Rock 25   Pickwick Beer 35   Coors Beer 25
Lime Ricky 25   Falstaff Beer 30

Outside Tray Service 25 Cents Extra—Between 11 and 2, 50 Cents
No Service Less Than 25c

A BRIEF HISTORY
OF WARNER BROS. STUDIOS

THERE IS A MOMENT in the PBS-produced documentary series *You Must Remember This*, a decade-by-decade history of Warner Bros. Studios, in which esteemed film critic Richard Schickel states, "The history of Warner Bros. is the history of Hollywood." From *The Jazz Singer*, the first talking picture, to Best Picture Oscar® winners like *The Life of Emile Zola*, *My Fair Lady*, *Chariots of Fire*, *Driving Miss Daisy*, *Unforgiven*, *Million Dollar Baby*, and *The Departed*, and including movies that were filmed primarily on the lot like *Casablanca* and *Argo* (honored by the Made in Hollywood award), Warner Bros. Studios has made an indelible mark in both global entertainment and popular culture.

HUMBLE BEGINNINGS

IT ALL BEGAN WITH four brothers from Ohio. Like many studio executives from the golden age of Hollywood, the Warner brothers came from a European Jewish family of modest means. Their parents, Benjamin and Pearl Wonskolaser, came to the United States in the late 1880s to build a better life for their 12 children (seven boys and five girls). They settled in Youngstown, Ohio, and changed their last name to the more American-sounding Warner. In 1903, four of the boys—Harry, Albert ("Abe"), Sam, and Jack—sold their family's horse to purchase a Kinetoscope, which was a portable film projector invented by Thomas Edison. The brothers traveled from town to town promoting their small, burgeoning "motion picture" business. After a few years, the brothers realized that distributing films would likely be the road to success, and soon they were distributing 200 films up and down the East Coast.

By 1918, it was clear to the four Warner brothers that they wanted to make original films as well. To do this, they moved to Los Angeles and set up shop in Hollywood, where the film industry was growing at a rapid pace. Warner Bros. Studios officially incorporated in Hollywood in 1923. The early success of *Rin Tin Tin*, featuring the first canine movie star, kept the studio afloat for the first few years while the brothers experimented with other original film projects and ideas.

On a visit to New York City in 1925, Sam and Harry Warner visited Bell Labs. They found an experimental sound system that synchronized a motion picture projector with a phonograph record, producing what came to be known as a "talking picture." The astute entrepreneurs knew this new invention, which was called a Vitaphone, was a game-changing piece of filmmaking hardware. They had to have it.

After securing the rights to the Vitaphone technology from Bell Labs, the brothers set off to work on the first film production with synchronized dialogue and musical sequencing, *The Jazz Singer*, starring Al Jolson, the biggest Broadway star of his era. When the film was released in 1927, it became Hollywood's first bona fide blockbuster. Sadly, Sam Warner, who played a seminal role in developing the Vitaphone system, died of pneumonia the night before *The Jazz Singer* premiered. But his legacy was clear: *The Jazz Singer* and the introduction of sound into motion pictures revolutionized the film industry. Once a scrappy upstart, Warner Bros. soon ruled the day with its "talkies," largely due to the brothers believing in innovation and a forward-thinking approach to the evolving industry.

FROM THE DEPRESSION TO WORLD WAR II AND ITS AFTERMATH: THE 1930s—1950s

DURING THE GREAT DEPRESSION, Warner Bros. Studios began to refine its movie-making style and produced numerous gangster films featuring Jimmy Cagney and Edward G. Robinson. Each Warner Bros. movie was meant to evoke what Harry Warner referred to as "The Three E's." "A Warner Bros. film," he commented, "should educate, entertain, and enlighten the viewing public." According to author and biographer Neal Gabler, Warner Bros. films exhibited "a style that was particularly appropriate for a certain kind of material—contemporary and urban—and those were the properties to which the studio gravitated, both by temperament and necessity."

Another big development in the Warner Bros. brand was the creation of the Looney Tunes and Merrie Melodies cartoons. As the Great Depression wore on, the cartoon characters we've all come to love, many of them drawn by animators Chuck Jones and Friz Freleng and voiced by Mel Blanc, cheered up audiences nationwide. Bugs Bunny, Daffy Duck, Elmer Fudd, Porky Pig, Tweety Bird and Sylvester, Wile E. Coyote and the Road Runner, and many other Looney Tunes characters continue to this day to entertain children and adults alike.

Warner Bros. films often supported the underdogs. "One could see the conscience at work, if less palpably, in dozens of films that embraced the losers and the loners, the prizefighters, meat packers, truck drivers, coal miners, cardsharps, gumshoes, racketeers, con artists, and the rest of what might have seemed like the detritus of Depression America," Gabler illustrates. "These were Warners' heroes, and Warners' films demonstrated an unusual sympathy for these people and their plight, so much so that they became favorite targets for outraged moralists who attacked them not only for depicting antisocial behavior, but for seeming to condone it." Harry Warner responded to this criticism directly, saying, "The motion picture presents right and wrong, as does the Bible. By showing both right and wrong, we teach the right."

Never was this more true than in the years leading up to World War II. Not only were the Warner brothers staunchly anti-fascist, they were the only major studio in Hollywood to make an anti-Nazi film (*Confessions of a Nazi Spy*) before the United States officially entered the war. In 1937, Warner Bros. Studios won its first Best Picture Academy Award for *The Life of Emile Zola*, starring Paul Muni in a fictionalized biopic about the French author. The film exposed the rampant anti-Semitism that existed in France in the late 1800s and early 1900s, and which was also recurring in Europe at the time the film was made.

The 1940s were probably the most prolific period for the studio: 40 original films were produced each year, including Best Picture Oscar® winner *Casablanca* and a string of critically acclaimed movies such as *The Maltese Falcon, The Treasure of the Sierra Madre, The Big Sleep,* and *Mildred Pierce,* a classic film noir for which Joan Crawford won the Academy Award for Best Actress in 1946.

More than anything, however, Hollywood in the forties belonged to Humphrey Bogart. It's impossible to recall a movie actor who, decades later, still personifies the turbulent forties better than Bogie. An actor who looked equally tough with or without a gun, Bogart started out in the 1930s as a character actor with bit roles in Warner Bros.' gangster movies. After director John Huston cast Bogart as detective Sam Spade in 1941's *The Maltese Falcon,* based on the popular Dashiell Hammett novel, Bogie became Hollywood's go-to leading man. The classic 1943 film *Casablanca,* in which Bogart most famously starred opposite Ingrid Bergman as a nightclub owner in the titular Moroccan city during World War II, never goes out of style. During the filming of Howard Hawks' adaptation of Ernest Hemingway's short novel *To Have and Have Not,* Bogart fell in love with his costar, actress Lauren Bacall. Marrying shortly thereafter in

1945, the couple displayed their on-screen chemistry in several subsequent films, most notably in Hawks' *The Big Sleep* and Huston's *Key Largo*.

Three benchmark films helped to define Warner Bros. Studios in the early 1950s: *A Streetcar Named Desire* (1951), starring a young Marlon Brando and Vivien Leigh in Elia Kazan's film adaptation of Tennessee Williams' Pulitzer Prize–winning play; Nicholas Ray's *Rebel Without a Cause* (1951), which featured *Giant* and *East of Eden* star James Dean in the role that would immortalize his legacy after a tragic car crash ended his life at the age of 24; and in 1954, George Cukor's *A Star is Born* portrayed Judy Garland as a young actress in Hollywood on her way up and James Mason as a famous film star on his way down.

Warner Bros. Studios also made the first successful 3-D horror film in the fifties—another significant technical innovation—with *House of Wax* (1953), starring horror legend Vincent Price. Toward the end of the decade, the studio released what many consider to have been two of the best westerns ever made: John Ford's *The Searchers* (1956), starring John Wayne, and Howard Hawks' *Rio Bravo* (1959), also starring John Wayne along with Dean Martin and Ricky Nelson.

When television became the dominant new medium in the 1950s, Warner Bros. embraced innovation once again. The studio created a television division and began producing shows on the Burbank lot, including *Cheyenne*, the first hour-long dramatic western series that aired for seven seasons. Several other western series followed, including *Maverick*, starring James Garner in the role that would launch his career.

ENTERING THE MODERN AGE: THE 1960s THROUGH THE 1990s

THE 1960S MARKED THE last time the studio was run by any of the actual Warner brothers, with Jack at the helm for much of the decade. In 1960, Frank Sinatra and his Las Vegas buddies were immortalized on celluloid in the Rat Pack crime caper, *Ocean's 11*. (Director Steven Soderbergh and producer Jerry Weintraub would resurrect the franchise featuring an all-star cast, led by George Clooney as Danny Ocean, with *Ocean's Eleven* in 2001, which was followed by two sequels.) In 1964, *My Fair Lady*, starring Audrey Hepburn and Rex Harrison, captivated both audiences and Academy members, winning eight Oscars®, including Best Picture.

Two years later, as sixties-era counterculture began to emerge, popular audience tastes started to shift as well. This was the so-called "New Hollywood," which addressed complex social issues and did not shy away from violence. Amidst an evolving industry landscape following the recently abolished Production Code, Warner Bros. Studios was yet again on the cutting edge with Mike Nichols' 1966 film adaptation of Edward Albee's Tony Award–winning play, *Who's Afraid of Virginia Woolf?*, starring Elizabeth Taylor and Richard Burton as a married couple on the rocks. The following year, 1967, was not only known as the "Summer of Love" in San Francisco, but also as the year "New Hollywood" really took off, largely because of one landmark film: *Bonnie and Clyde*, directed by Arthur Penn and starring Warren Beatty and Faye Dunaway as the fabled Depression-era bank robbers Clyde Barrow and Bonnie Parker. This film, while extremely violent for its time, received rave reviews and ushered in a groundbreaking new era in movie making.

The 1971 film *Dirty Harry*, starring Clint Eastwood, was one of the studio's biggest successes since *Bonnie and Clyde*. It also signaled the beginning of a long and fruitful relationship with Eastwood. "I believe I've been on the lot longer than any other actor or director in its long history, though I've never had a long-term contract with the studio," Eastwood wrote in the book compendium to the documentary series, *You Must Remember This*. "We just go from picture to picture, trusting one another and liking one another. Through the years I've done films at other studios, but at Warner Bros. four different management teams have

given me the freedom to make the films I've wanted to make—even sometimes when we all knew they would not be huge winners at the box office. It's a way of doing business that is, sadly, no longer common in the movie industry."

The seventies also saw studio chief John Calley and reclusive filmmaker Stanley Kubrick form a successful partnership. In 1971, Warner Bros. released Kubrick's *A Clockwork Orange*, the dystopian tale of thuggery and ultra-violence based on the novel by Anthony Burgess. In 1973, Martin Scorsese cowrote and directed *Mean Streets*, his first major feature film, based on his personal experiences growing up in New York City's Little Italy neighborhood. In that same year, William Friedkin's *The Exorcist* broke box office records, and Bruce Lee's *Enter the Dragon* was completed, although Lee died suddenly of a brain aneurysm before the film's release. Warner Bros. released Kubrick's next film, the period drama *Barry Lyndon*, which received four Academy Awards in 1975, while Richard Donner successfully rebooted *Superman* into a film series in 1978 starring Christopher Reeve.

In the eighties, Warner Bros. released several noteworthy films, including 1982's science fiction masterpiece *Blade Runner*, directed by Ridley Scott, and *Chariots of Fire*, which won the Best Picture Oscar® in 1982. *The Color Purple*, based on Alice Walker's Pulitzer Prize–winning novel set in the American South and directed by Steven Spielberg, was released in 1985 and was nominated for 11 Academy Awards. Mel Gibson and Danny Glover starred as Los Angeles detectives in 1987's blockbuster hit *Lethal Weapon*, which led to three sequels. Michael Keaton portrayed the title character in two of director Tim Burton's breakthrough films, first in *Beetlejuice* in 1988 and a year later in 1989's *Batman*, the first feature film about the caped crusader. Warner Bros. ended the eighties with a come-from-behind win for the Best Picture Oscar® for *Driving Miss Daisy*, starring Jessica Tandy as a charming but cantankerous Southern grandmother and the now-ubiquitous Morgan Freeman as her chauffeur.

Two important mergers occurred in 1989 and 1990 to expand the breadth of the company and spur a period of further growth. In January 1990, Warner Communications, Inc., the parent company of Warner Bros. Studios, merged with Time, Inc., the global magazine and book publishing company that owned several cable television outlets, including Home Box Office (HBO). The combined company, known as Time Warner, Inc., formed one of the largest media and entertainment companies in the world.

The other merger took place in 1989, but began to make a significant impact in the 1990s, when Warner Communications, Inc. acquired Lorimar Telepictures, one of the most prolific and highly regarded television production companies of the day. Lorimar's tradition of innovative, quality programming included *The Waltons, Dallas, Knots Landing, Falcon Crest, Eight is Enough, Full House, Perfect Strangers,* and *Family Matters.* The merger paved the way for several classic television shows to be developed, including *Friends, The West Wing,* and *ER* (which have collectively garnered more than 50 Emmys), all of which were shot on the Warner Bros. lot in Burbank. In 1995, Warner Bros. Studios added to its reach with the launch of the company's first (and the nation's fifth) television network, initially called The WB and now known as The CW, jointly owned with CBS. Also in the mid-nineties, Warner Bros. and Time Warner, along with Toshiba and several other consumer electronics companies, were instrumental in the development and standardization of the DVD format, another historic innovation for the studio.

On the feature film side, the studio began the 1990s by producing several Oscar®-nominated films, such as *JFK, The Fugitive,* and Scorsese's *Goodfellas*. And 1992 was the year in which Clint Eastwood returned to glory with a new type of western in *Unforgiven,* which won four Academy Awards, including Best Director for Eastwood and Best

Picture. In 1995, Michael Mann's *Heat* brought Robert DeNiro and Al Pacino together in a crime drama set in Los Angeles, while director Curtis Hanson dished up 1997's retro-noir *LA Confidential*, based on the book by crime writer James Ellroy recalling Los Angeles in the 1950s. At the end of the 1990s, the Wachowski siblings struck a chord with a sci-fi allegory about true consciousness in *The Matrix*, which was not only a smash hit at the box office and inspired two sequels but garnered widespread critical praise as well—including four Academy Awards.

WARNER BROS. STUDIOS ENTERS THE 21ST CENTURY ON A WAVE OF FANTASY

THE FIRST DECADE of the new millennium was, for the studio, the Harry Potter era. Based on the wildly popular books written by J. K. Rowling, Warner Bros. produced eight Harry Potter films, all shot at Leavesden Studios in England (now Warner Bros. Studios Leavesden). Also during this period, Peter Jackson's epic *Lord of the Rings* trilogy, based on the books by J.R.R. Tolkien, was produced by sister company New Line Cinema. The final *Lord of the Rings* movie won the Best Picture Oscar® in 2003. The *Lord of the Rings* series was followed more recently by a prequel film trilogy based on Tolkien's novel, *The Hobbit*.

Other fantasy films followed. Christopher Nolan reimagined Batman's origin story when he cowrote, directed, and produced *The Dark Knight* trilogy (2005, 2008, and 2012), which collectively broke box office records worldwide. Nolan also wrote and directed the critically acclaimed sci-fi thriller *Inception* (2010), another major box office success featuring an ensemble cast led by Leonardo DiCaprio, Marion Cotillard, Joseph Gordon-Levitt, Ellen Page, Ken Watanabe, Cillian Murphy, Tom Hardy, Tom Berenger, and Michael Caine.

Interspersed among the epic fantasy worlds, Warner Bros. released 2004's *Million Dollar Baby*, which earned Eastwood his second Best Picture and

Best Director Oscars®. Following this critical success in 2006, the studio released another Academy Award–winning film, *The Departed*, which took home the Best Picture Oscar® and also earned Scorsese his first and only Best Director Academy Award. In 2012, George Clooney and Grant Heslov collaborated with Ben Affleck to produce *Argo*, which was also directed by and starred Affleck. *Argo* took home several Academy Awards that year, including the Best Picture Oscar®. The following year, Alfonso Cuarón directed the critically and commercially lauded *Gravity*, starring Sandra Bullock and George Clooney. The film won seven Academy Awards, including Cuarón's first for Best Director. In 2014, Warner Bros. continued producing quality films, with Eastwood's highly successful and critically acclaimed *American Sniper*, starring Bradley Cooper. *The LEGO Movie* also became one of the surprise hits of the year, pushing the boundaries of animated films further than the originators of Looney Tunes could ever have imagined and spawning a whole new movie franchise.

Popular television shows produced by Warner Bros. since 2000 include *Gilmore Girls, Smallville, Supernatural, The Mentalist, Two and a Half Men, One Tree Hill,* and *Gossip Girl.* As this book goes to print, *The Ellen DeGeneres Show, Conan, Pretty Little Liars,* and Chuck Lorre's *The Big Bang Theory* are some of the most popular television shows currently shooting on the lot.

But if you walk south on the Burbank lot toward Mount Lee and squint ever so slightly between the old sound stages near the front gate around dusk, it's not hard to conjure up an image of Jimmy Cagney or Humphrey Bogart disappearing into the fog. As you hum the opening bars of "As Time Goes By," you must remember this: Hollywood history continues to be made at Warner Bros. Studios every day.

Thai-Style Chicken Skewers with Peanut Sauce

Seafood Ceviche

Heirloom Tomato Crab Salad

Maryland Blue Crab Cakes

Burrata Crostini with Fig-Olive Tapenade

Hamachi Crudo

Lobster Corn Dogs

Pan con Tomate

Ahi Tuna Tostada

Roasted Baby Vegetables

Duck Confit Flautas

Artichokes Romana

Bloody Mary Shrimp Cocktail

Beef Sliders

Seared Scallops with Black Garlic Puree

Prosciutto and Melon

Steak Tartare

APPETIZERS

How to kick off a meal, Warner Bros. Studios style? Start with the best possible ingredients and prepare them with a dash of creativity. At the commissary, olive tapenade is spiked with black mission figs and served with creamy burrata cheese; corn dogs are fancified with lobster; candied jalapeño adds subtle heat to hamachi crudo. Avocado espuma takes ahi tuna tostadas to the next level. There are ways to start simply—a mélange of roasted farmers' market vegetables, artichokes prepared Roman-style—or kick things off with a bang (duck confit flautas, anyone?). Whether you're grilling mushroom tartines for a low-key lunch or prepping pan con tomate for a celebration, the recipes that follow provide an unforgettable beginning to any meal.

makes two servings

2	**Tablespoons creamy peanut butter**
2	**Tablespoons plus 2 teaspoons low-sodium soy sauce**
	Juice of 1 lime
	Juice of ½ small lemon
1	**Teaspoon light brown sugar**
2	**Teaspoons curry powder**
2	**Garlic cloves, peeled and minced**
½	**Teaspoon Sriracha**
2	**6-ounce boneless, skinless chicken breasts**
1	**Stem green onion, sliced**
	Wooden skewers, for grilling

Thai-Style Chicken Skewers with Peanut Sauce

In a mixing bowl, combine peanut butter, soy sauce, lime juice, lemon juice, brown sugar, curry powder, garlic, and Sriracha. Mix well and let stand. Divide mixture into 2 even batches using a separate bowl.

Cut each chicken breast into 3 2-ounce strips and weave onto skewers. Place chicken skewers in 1 batch of peanut sauce, cover completely, and refrigerate for at least 2 hours (overnight is best). When ready, heat your grill on high. Grill skewers until fully cooked through, approximately 5 minutes. Serve with clean batch of peanut sauce and garnish with sliced green onion.

makes four servings

	Juice of 5 limes
½	**Tablespoon lemon zest**
	Juice of 3 lemons
1	**Large clove garlic, smashed and minced**
½	**Jalapeño, minced**
3	**Ounces cleaned bay scallops**
3	**Ounces 21/25-count shrimp, roughly chopped**
3	**Ounces red snapper, roughly chopped**
½	**Red onion, ⅛-inch diced**
2	**Heaping tablespoons finely chopped cilantro**
2	**Tablespoons ⅛-inch diced red bell pepper**
2	**Tablespoons ⅛-inch diced yellow bell pepper**
½	**Tablespoon Tajin chile-lime salt* (can substitute Kosher salt)**
2	**Tablespoons extra-virgin olive oil**
	Chile thread, for garnish,* optional
	Tortilla chips, for serving

Seafood Ceviche

In a large mixing bowl, combine lime juice, lemon zest, lemon juice, garlic, and jalapeño. Let sit for 10 minutes. Add scallops, shrimp, and snapper and stir to combine. Let mixture sit, stirring every 15 minutes, until semi-opaque (about 1 hour). Add onion, cilantro, bell peppers, and Tajin. Continue stirring every 10 minutes until fish is completely opaque— about 30 to 45 minutes more.

Place in refrigerator for an hour to chill. Remove from fridge and fold in extra-virgin olive oil.

To serve, place ½ cup ceviche in a small bowl and garnish with chile threads. Serve with tortilla chips.

* available in specialty Mexican markets

Chive Oil
makes approximately one cup

1 Bunch (approximately ½ cup) chives
1 Cup extra-virgin olive oil

¼ Teaspoon kosher salt

Bring a pot of water to a boil and prepare an ice bath. Blanch chives for 10 seconds, then shock in ice bath and roughly chop. Place chives in blender with 1 tablespoon ice water and blend on high until just pureed—about 45 seconds (do not over-blend or chives will turn brown). Transfer puree to a bowl. Whisk in oil and salt, and let rest in a sealed container for 2 hours before use. (Note: The longer you store the Chive Oil, the darker it will look and the more intense the flavor will become.)

Heirloom Tomato Crab Salad

Place crab into large mixing bowl and discard any shells or cartilage. Add chives, onions, bell pepper, mayonnaise, and lime juice and season with salt and pepper to taste. Stir well to combine; if too dry, add more mayonnaise, bit by bit. To serve, place a 2½-inch by 3-inch ring mold in center of plate and set ½ cup crab mixture inside. Using a spoon, gently pat down sides and remove the mold. Encircle the crab mixture with 7 heirloom tomatoes (14 halves) per plate (tomatoes should overlap slightly). In a small mixing bowl, gently toss petite greens and Citrus Vinaigrette. Place a small handful atop crab, garnish with Chive Oil, and serve.

makes six servings

1	Pound fresh Maryland jumbo lump blue crab meat (substitute Dungeness if not available)
¼	Cup chopped chives
¼	Cup chopped green onion
¼	Cup minced red onion
¼	Cup minced red and yellow pepper
1	Cup mayonnaise
	Juice of 3 limes
	Sea salt and black pepper, to taste
42	Heirloom teardrop tomatoes, halved
1	Container petite greens
4	Tablespoons Citrus Vinaigrette *(recipe on page 97)*
½	Teaspoon Chive Oil, for garnish

Maryland Blue Crab Cakes

Place crab into large mixing bowl and discard any shells or cartilage. Add remaining ingredients except for the panko and extra-virgin olive oil and mix well. Add ½ cup panko and stir again. Pour the remaining panko into a bowl. Form the crab into small patties—about 2¼ ounces each—and roll in panko until evenly coated. Place crab cakes on a tray and reserve in the refrigerator for at least 1 hour before cooking. Heat extra-virgin olive oil in a sauté pan and sauté the crab cakes for 2½ minutes per side. Serve with lemon wedges.

makes three servings
(two small crab cakes each)

1	Pound fresh Maryland jumbo lump blue crab meat (substitute Dungeness if not available)
¼	Cup chopped chives
¼	Cup chopped green onion (white and light green parts)
¼	Cup minced red onion
¼	Cup minced red and yellow bell pepper (about half of each pepper)
2	Tablespoons Sambal chili-garlic sauce
1½	Cups mayonnaise
	Juice of 3 limes
1	Pound panko bread crumbs
1	Tablespoon extra-virgin olive oil
	Lemon wedges

Fig-Olive Tapenade
makes approximately two cups

1 Basket / 16 Ounces fresh, ripe Black Mission figs, de-stemmed and halved
½ Cup pitted Kalamata olives, halved

½ Tablespoon rosemary, minced
⅓ Cup extra-virgin olive oil (preferably Arbequina)
¼ Cup Balsamic Syrup *(recipe on facing page)*

Place figs, olives, and rosemary in a food processor and pulse until the mixture is well chopped and incorporated; it should be the texture of coarse jam. Turn out into a bowl, add extra-virgin olive oil and Balsamic Syrup and stir to combine. The tapenade will last in the refrigerator for up to 3 weeks.

Burrata Crostini with Fig-Olive Tapenade

makes two servings

8	**Slices baguette, cut on the bias**
	Extra-virgin olive oil, for brushing bread
4	**Tablespoons Fig-Olive Tapenade**
8	**Tablespoons burrata cheese**
	Sea salt and black pepper
8	**Leaves arugula**
1	**Tablespoon peppery, fruity extra-virgin olive oil**
½	**Teaspoon olive oil (preferably Frantoio), for garnish**

Preheat oven to 400°F. Brush bread with extra-virgin olive oil and toast for 5 to 6 minutes until golden-brown. Top each piece of bread with ½ tablespoon tapenade, 1 tablespoon burrata, a sprinkle of salt and pepper, and 1 arugula leaf. Place on a serving platter and drizzle with the tablespoon of fruity extra-virgin olive oil.

Hamachi Crudo

makes two servings

6	**Ounces Japanese hamachi (yellowtail), thinly sliced**
½	**Teaspoon Togarashi,* optional**
1	**Teaspoon Candied Jalapeño**
10	**Sprigs micro cilantro, or 5 cilantro leaves**
2	**Teaspoons ponzu,* optional**
1	**Teaspoon yuzu pearls,* optional (can substitute a squeeze of lemon)**
4	**Tablespoons watermelon radish, julienned paper-thin on mandoline**
	Basil Oil *(recipe on page 41)*

*available in specialty Asian markets

Arrange hamachi slices on a rectangular plate; season with Togarashi. Drizzle Candied Jalapeño (in its simple syrup) over top. Garnish with cilantro, ponzu, watermelon radish, and yuzu pearls and finish with a drizzle of Basil Oil.

Candied Jalapeño
makes approximately two cups

8 Jalapenos, sliced paper-thin
Zest from 1 lemon
Juice of 2 lemons

3 Cups sugar
4 Cups water

Place all ingredients in a 3-quart pot over high heat. Bring to a robust simmer; continue simmering until liquid is reduced by almost half, or until thick enough to coat the back of a spoon—about 12 minutes. When ready, jalapeños should be soft. Remove from heat and let cool, then refrigerate. If too thick to drizzle upon serving, loosen with hot water.

Balsamic Syrup
makes one cup

2 Cups balsamic vinegar **½ Cup brown sugar**

In a small saucepan over medium heat, stir vinegar and sugar until sugar is dissolved. Turn the heat to high, bring to a boil, and then reduce heat to low and simmer until the liquid is reduced by half—about 20 minutes. It's ready when the liquid is glaze-like and coats the back of a spoon. Let cool, pour into a lidded jar or bottle, and store in the refrigerator.

Basil Oil

makes approximately one cup

1½ Cups basil leaves
¼ Cup packed flat-leaf (Italian)
  parsley leaves

1 Cup extra-virgin olive oil

Bring a large saucepan of salted water to a boil and prepare an ice bath. Blanch herbs for 15 seconds, then immediately transfer to ice bath to cool. Drain and coarsely chop. Squeeze out excess water with paper towels. Add herbs and oil to blender. Puree for 3 to 4 minutes, or until bright green. Pour into a jar or other airtight container, cover, and refrigerate for 1 day. Strain oil through cheesecloth and refrigerate for another 24 hours. Bring oil to room temperature before serving.

Lobster Corn Dogs

Add onion, celery, bay leaves, lemon, and parsley to an 8-quart stockpot filled with water and bring to a boil. Prepare an ice bath. Add lobster to stockpot and boil for 7½ minutes, then remove and chill in ice bath for 4 minutes. Once cool, break apart claws and tail and extract meat. Cut tail meat and claws into 1-inch by 1-inch pieces (save any trimmings and knuckle meat for another use).

In a mixing bowl, combine cornmeal (or polenta), flour, sugar, baking powder, and salt and and stir until combined. Add milk and egg and stir again. Test for thickness; the batter should fully coat a spoon. If too thick, add milk to adjust.

Gently skewer 1 lobster piece on each stick. Heat canola oil to 350°F in a deep fryer or stock pot. Dredge skewered lobster into batter and drip off excess. Drop whole skewers in oil and fry until golden brown—about 2 minutes. Remove with tongs and drain skewers on a paper towel. To serve, smear 1 tablespoon grain mustard on each plate with the back of a spoon. Place skewer on top and garnish with microgreens.

makes four servings

1	Medium onion, chopped
3	Stalks celery, chopped
2	Bay leaves
	Juice of 1 lemon
1	Bunch parsley
1½	Pounds live Maine lobster
1	Cup plus 2 tablespoons yellow cornmeal or polenta
1½	Cup all-purpose flour
½	Cup granulated sugar
1½	Tablespoons baking powder
	Kosher salt
2	Cups whole milk
1	Whole egg plus 1 egg yolk
4	6-inch wooden skewers
4	Cups canola oil
4	Tablespoons grain mustard
1	Package microgreens, for garnish

Pan con Tomate

In a food processor, combine tomatoes, garlic, salt, vinegar, and pepper. Pulse about 10 times, for 3 seconds at a time, while slowly drizzling in extra-virgin olive oil. The consistency shouldn't be entirely smooth—just bound by the extra-virgin olive oil. Chill for 45 minutes. To serve, toast baguette slices in oven, spoon 1 tablespoon tomato mixture onto each piece, and garnish with basil.

makes six servings

8	Medium tomatoes, roughly chopped
4	Garlic cloves, chopped
1	Teaspoon sea salt
1	Teaspoon red wine vinegar
	Black pepper, to taste
¾	Cup Arbequina olive oil
1	Baguette, cut into 24 pieces on the bias
1	Package micro basil, for garnish, or 12 basil leaves, julienned

Avocado Espuma
makes approximately one cup

2 Avocados, peeled, pitted, and chopped
½ Jalapeño, peeled and chopped
¼ Bunch cilantro, stems removed
Juice of ½ lemon

Juice of 1 lime
¼ Cup heavy cream
½ Teaspoon sugar
1 Tablespoon salt

In a blender, puree avocado, jalapeño, cilantro, and citrus juices. With the blender running, add cream and process until smooth. Season with sugar and salt. Reserve in refrigerator until ready to use.

Ahi Tuna Tostada

In a 2-quart saucepan, add oil and bring to 325°F. Using a 2-inch ring mold or cookie cutter, cut 4 rings out of the corn tortilla. Drop into the hot oil and fry until crispy—about 1½ minutes. Drain on paper towels, season with salt, and set aside to cool.

In a stainless steel mixing bowl, add the remaining ingredients except cilantro and Avocado Espuma and mix well. Place a small amount of mixture onto each tortilla circle. Garnish with a dollop of Avocado Espuma and a sprig of micro cilantro.

makes two servings

2	Cups canola oil
2	Corn tortillas
	Sea salt
8	Ounces ahi tuna, diced into ¼-inch cubes
½	Teaspoon Togarashi,* optional
½	Teaspoon shallots, minced
½	Teaspoon chives, minced
2	Tablespoons ponzu,* optional
2	Teaspoons Sriracha
8	Sprigs micro cilantro or 4 cilantro leaves
	Avocado Espuma

available in specialty Asian markets

Roasted Baby Vegetables

Preheat oven to 450°F. Fill a medium-sized saucepan with water and bring to a boil. Add shallots and boil for 1 minute. Drain and rinse shallots under cold water. Using a sharp paring knife, trim the root ends and peel. If shallots are small, leave whole; if they're large, cut in half length-wise.

In a large bowl, combine shallots, carrots, squash, oil, salt, pepper, rosemary, 1 teaspoon vinegar, and 1 tablespoon parsley, and toss to coat well. Spread the vegetables in a single layer on a large baking sheet. Roast, turning the vegetables twice, until tender and lightly browned in spots—about 30 minutes.

Transfer the vegetables to a large bowl, discarding the rosemary stems. Drizzle with a bit more extra-virgin olive oil and the remaining teaspoon of vinegar. Garnish with the remaining tablespoon of parsley.

makes four servings

1½	Cups whole shallots, unpeeled
2	Cups young carrots, with ¼ inch of greens left attached, or baby carrots
1½	Cups baby yellow summer squash
1	Tablespoon extra-virgin olive oil
½	Teaspoon salt
	Black pepper, to taste
10	Sprigs fresh rosemary
2	Teaspoons cider vinegar
2	Tablespoons fresh flat-leaf (Italian) parsley, chopped

Cabbage Slaw
makes four servings

¼ **Purple cabbage head, shredded**
¼ **Green cabbage head, shredded**
¼ **Napa cabbage head, shredded**
2 **Roma tomatoes, diced**
½ **Yellow onion, diced**
½ **Bunch cilantro, chopped**

Juice of ½ lemon
2 **Tablespoons extra-virgin olive oil**
Juice of 1 lime
¼ **Cup queso ranchero, crumbled**
Sea salt and black pepper, to taste

Place all ingredients into a mixing bowl. Toss thoroughly and let sit for 20 minutes. Toss again and let sit for 10 minutes more (this process softens the cabbage); season with salt and pepper to taste.

makes four servings

4	**Duck legs**
1½	**Tablespoons kosher salt**
½	**Teaspoon black pepper**
10	**Cloves garlic, smashed**
4	**Bay leaves**
5	**Sprigs thyme**
5	**Sprigs rosemary**
6	**Cups extra-virgin olive oil**
2	**Cups grated smoked cheddar cheese**
⅓	**Cup chopped scallions**
1	**4-ounce can chipotles in adobo sauce, pureed**
10	**6-inch flour tortillas, warmed**
10	**Toothpicks**
	Cabbage Slaw
	Avocado Espuma, for garnish
	(recipe on page 45)

makes four servings

2	**Large artichokes**
1	**Lemon, halved**
1	**Cup fresh bread crumbs**
3	**Tablespoons grated Parmesan cheese**
1	**Large clove garlic, finely chopped**
1	**Tablespoon fresh flat-leaf (Italian) parsley, finely chopped**
½	**Tablespoon grated lemon zest**
¼	**Tablespoon shallot, minced**
	Sea salt and black pepper
½	**Tablespoon extra-virgin olive oil**
½	**Cup dry white wine**
½	**Cup plus 1 to 2 tablespoons vegetable or chicken stock or broth**

Duck Confit Flautas

Place 2 duck legs skin side down in snug, high-walled dish. Season with salt and black pepper. Place garlic, bay leaves, thyme, and rosemary over the legs; place the remaining 2 leg portions, skin side up, on top. Cover duck legs with ½ cup extra-virgin olive oil (or more, if needed, as the legs should be entirely covered). Cover the dish and refrigerate for 4 hours.

Preheat oven to 235°F. Remove duck from refrigerator; place legs in a deep braising pan, skin-side down, and cover with remaining 5½ cups extra-virgin olive oil. Cover and roast until the meat pulls away from the bone—9 to 12 hours. Remove from the oven and let cool for about 1 hour. Remove legs from oil. Cut meat from bones and transfer to a bowl. Add cheese, scallions, and pureed chipotles and mix well.

Increase oven to 350°F. Place 6 tablespoons of duck-cheese mixture in a line down the center of each tortilla and roll the tortilla around it, sealing the end with a toothpick. Transfer to an oiled baking dish and bake until crispy—about 8 to 10 minutes. (Alternately, you can fry the flautas at 350°F for 2½ minutes.) Let cool and cut in half on the bias. Serve 5 pieces per plate, garnished with Avocado Espuma and Cabbage Slaw.

Artichokes Romana

Preheat oven to 350°F. Prepare the artichokes by removing the tough outer leaves and trimming the stalks. Open the leaves and pull out the furry choke. Fill a bowl with water and squeeze the lemon halves into the water; add the artichokes (to prevent them from browning).

Mix breadcrumbs and Parmesan with garlic, parsley, lemon zest, and shallot. Press the mixture firmly into the hollow of each artichoke. Season with salt and black pepper and place, stuffed-side up, in a deep, oven-proof dish. Add a splash of oil, then add the white wine and stock.

Cover the dish and bake for 1 hour, or until almost all of the liquid has evaporated and the artichokes can be easily pierced with a knife.

Bloody Mary Shrimp Cocktail

Place the halved lemon, onion, and celery stalks in a large pot of water and bring to a boil; meanwhile, prepare an ice bath. Add shrimp and boil until they turn opaque—3 to 4 minutes. Cool shrimp in ice bath, then drain and dry. Chill before serving.

In a blender, combine garlic, onion, cilantro, tomato juice, lime juice, Worcestershire, horseradish, jalapeño, brine, and tequila. Blend on high speed until fully incorporated. Taste and season with salt and pepper as needed; transfer to a bowl and gently stir in avocado.

To serve, spoon cocktail sauce into martini glasses and place shrimp around the glass (tails facing out). Garnish each glass with a lemon wedge and a celery leaf.

makes six servings

2	Lemons, 1 halved, 1 cut into 8 wedges, for garnish
1	Small onion, halved
1	Bunch celery, stalks roughly chopped, leaves reserved for garnish
32	Large (U10) bay tail-on shrimp, peeled and deveined
1	Tablespoon chopped garlic
½	Cup chopped red onion
¼	Cup chopped cilantro
1	Cup tomato juice
	Juice of 3 limes
1	Teaspoon Worcestershire sauce
¼	Cup prepared horseradish
1	Pickled jalapeño*
¼	Cup pickled jalapeño brine
2	Ounces reposado tequila
	Sea salt and black pepper
1	Avocado, diced

available in specialty markets

Beef Sliders

In a large bowl, mix ground beef, onion, and garlic. Season with salt and pepper, then form mixture into 4 2½-ounce patties.

Heat a large skillet to high. When ready, pan-sear patties until cooked on each side, approximately 3 minutes per side. Top each patty with a slice of cheese, turn off heat, and let melt, approximately 30 seconds.

Dab ketchup on bottom of each bun and set burger atop. Add pickle chip and top bun and serve.

makes two servings

10	Ounces ground Angus chuck
1	Teaspoon minced onion
¼	Teaspoon minced garlic
4	Pickle chips
1	Large square slice of Tillamook cheddar cheese, quartered
1	Tablespoon plus 1 teaspoon ketchup
4	Mini Hawaiian burger buns or brioche dinner rolls
	Sea salt and black pepper, to taste

Seared Scallops with Black Garlic Puree

In a blender, combine black garlic, ½ cup warm water, and 3 tablespoons oil. Puree on low speed until combined then blend on medium for 1 minute more until smooth. Reserve at room temperature.

In a pot over high heat, bring kumquats, sugar, and 3 cups water to a boil. Reduce to a high simmer and cook until kumquats are soft and mixture is syrupy—about 30 to 40 minutes. Remove compote from heat and let cool slightly.

Season scallops with salt and pepper. Heat 2 tablespoons oil in a large sauté pan over high heat and sear scallops on 1 side until golden brown—about 1½ minutes. Flip and sear for 2 additional minutes. Remove from heat.

Heat the remaining 1 tablespoon extra-virgin olive oil in a separate sauté pan over medium heat; add pea tendrils, season with salt and pepper, and sauté until just wilted—about 45 seconds.

To serve, place pea tendrils in 1 corner of a square plate. Drop 1 tablespoon of black garlic puree next to the tendrils then drag spoon in an upward motion to create a smear effect. Add 3 teaspoons kumquat compote next to tendrils in a triangle formation. Nestle 4 scallops per plate alongside and top with a drizzle of kumquat syrup (from the compote).

makes four servings

6	**Bulbs fermented black garlic, peeled*** **(can substitute roasted caramelized garlic)**
½	**Cup warm water**
6	**Tablespoons extra-virgin olive oil**
1	**Cup kumquats, halved**
1½	**Cups granulated sugar**
3	**Cups water**
16	**Large (U10) bay scallops**
	Sea salt and black pepper
2	**Cups packed pea tendrils, optional**

*available in specialty Asian markets

Prosciutto and Melon

Scoop 6 balls from each melon using a 1-inch melon baller. Run your fingers halfway up each rosemary sprig to strip the bottom half of each stalk. Wrap each melon ball with a slice of prosciutto, then use the rosemary as a skewer and stick it through the prosciutto-wrapped melon. Place skewers on a plate and drizzle with Fig Balsamic Syrup.

makes four servings	
½	**Cantaloupe**
½	**Honeydew**
2	**Ounces thinly sliced prosciutto**
12	**2-inch rosemary sprigs**
1	**Teaspoon Fig Balsamic Syrup**

Fig Balsamic Syrup
makes one quarter cup

3 Cups fig balsamic vinegar**   1 Small sprig rosemary
1 Tablespoon granulated sugar

Place ingredients in a medium saucepan over medium heat. Bring to a boil and then reduce to a simmer. Simmer uncovered until liquid reduces by ¾, or until you achieve a syrup-like consistency that coats the back of a spoon—about 30 minutes. Remove from heat and cool completely. If syrup is too thick, stir in hot water, a small amount at a time, until desired consistency is reached.

**optional, can substitute Balsamic vinegar for Balsamic Syrup recipe

Dijon Aioli
makes one quarter cup

2 Tablespoons mayonnaise	1 Tablespoon Dijon mustard
Juice of 1 lemon wedge	¼ Teaspoon minced garlic

Place ingredients in a mixing bowl and stir until thoroughly combined.

makes two servings

6	Slices baguette
1	Teaspoon extra-virgin olive oil
8	Ounces filet mignon, finely diced
1	Tablespoon flat-leaf (Italian) parsley, chopped
1	Teaspoon capers, chopped
1	Teaspoon Niçoise olives, chopped
1	Teaspoon shallots, finely minced
	Sea salt and black pepper
2	Teaspoons Dijon Aioli
2	Quail eggs (can substitute peewee egg)

Steak Tartare

Preheat oven to 350°F. Brush the baguette slices with extra-virgin olive oil, place in the oven and toast for 5 minutes. In a mixing bowl, combine steak, parsley, capers, olives, and shallots and season with salt and pepper. Divide between 2 serving plates. Place a heaping teaspoon of Dijon Aioli on the plate and drag the spoon through it to create a swoosh. In a small nonstick sauté pan with a drizzle of extra-virgin olive oil, fry quail eggs sunny-side up. Serve the quail eggs on top of the tartare.

Caesar Salad

Modern Italian Chop

Grilled Shrimp, Burrata, and Peaches

Bistro Steak Salad

Ahi Tuna Niçoise

Mediterranean Salad

White Bean Salad

Yellow Tomato Gazpacho

Beet Salad

Maine Lobster Cobb Salad

Sirloin Chili

SOUPS AND SALADS

After whetting their appetites, Warner Bros. Studios executives and talent feast on soups and salads bearing a hint of Mediterranean and a nod to classic Americana: a Caesar salad with decades of devotees, bowls of robust chili, crostini layered with prosciutto and juicy grilled peaches. In the summertime, you'll find bright yellow tomato gazpacho and Niçoise salad with seared ahi tuna and the season's freshest vegetables. Chillier months call for heartier fare: hanger steak topping arugula salad, while salami, garbanzos, and Provolone star in the modern Italian chop. Whatever the season or occasion, you'll find what you're looking for—you might even create a classic or two of your own.

Caesar Salad

makes four servings

3	**Romaine hearts, chopped**
½	**Cup Smoked Paprika Croutons**
¼	**Cup grated Parmesan cheese**
6	**Tablespoons Caesar Dressing**

In a large mixing bowl, combine lettuce, croutons, and cheese and toss to combine. Add dressing, toss thoroughly, and serve.

Smoked Paprika Croutons
makes two cups

½ Baguette, cut into ½-inch cubes
1 Tablespoon chopped garlic
1½ Tablespoons extra-virgin olive oil

¼ Teaspoon smoked paprika
Sea salt

Preheat oven to 350°F. In a bowl, combine bread, garlic, oil, paprika and a pinch of salt. Toss well, pour onto a baking sheet, and bake for approximately 30 minutes, or until crisp. Let cool before serving.

Caesar Dressing
makes one cup

¼ Cup grated Parmesan cheese
½ Cup mayonnaise
1 Teaspoon anchovy paste
½ Tablespoon balsamic vinegar

1½ Teaspoons Dijon mustard
⅛ Teaspoon black pepper
1 Teaspoon capers
⅛ Cup extra-virgin olive oil

In a blender, place all ingredients except extra-virgin olive oil and blend on medium speed until incorporated—about 2 minutes. Turn blender to high and slowly drizzle in oil until emulsified—about 1 minute. If mixture gets too thick, add a bit of cold water to loosen. Refrigerate at least 30 minutes before serving.

Modern Italian Chop

½	Cup Genoa salami, diced
6	Tablespoons diced provolone cheese
10	Kalamata olives, pitted
2	Teaspoons Arbequina olive oil
¼	Cup diced roasted red pepper
¼	Cup garbanzo beans
½	Cup plus 2 tablespoons diced Roma tomatoes
3	Marinated artichoke hearts, chopped
1	Tablespoon shaved red onion
6	Tablespoons diced cucumber
¼	Cup Red Wine Vinaigrette
4	Tablespoons petite greens

In a mixing bowl, combine all ingredients except the greens. Toss well, season with salt and pepper, and transfer to a serving bowl. Garnish with petite greens.

Red Wine Vinaigrette
makes three cups

¾ Cup red wine vinegar
Juice of ½ lemon
½ Teaspoon dry oregano
½ Teaspoon fresh garlic, chopped

2 Teaspoons sea salt
Black pepper, to taste
½ Teaspoons granulated sugar
2½ Cups extra-virgin olive oil

Place all ingredients except for extra-virgin olive oil in a blender. Turn the blender to medium speed and slowly add the extra-virgin olive oil. If the consistency is too thick, thin with small amounts of cold water. Dress salad. Extra dressing keeps in the refrigerator for up to a week.

Grilled Shrimp, Burrata, and Peaches

8	Large (U10) shrimp, peeled and deveined
1	Teaspoon chopped garlic
2	Teaspoons chopped parsley
¼	Cup extra-virgin olive oil
2	Ripe peaches, quartered
6	Ounces burrata cheese
	Sea salt and black pepper
1	Package microgreens, for garnish
1	Teaspoon Fig Balsamic Syrup, optional *(recipe on page 52)*
3	Teaspoons orange blossom honey, optional
1	Teaspoon Arbequina olive oil, for garnish

In a mixing bowl, combine garlic, parsley, and extra-virgin olive oil; add shrimp and gently toss. Cover and marinate for at least 30 minutes.

On a hot grill, grill peach quarters until grill marks form—about 2 minutes per side. Place in a small bowl and cover with plastic wrap. Remove shrimp from marinade and grill until opaque—about 3 minutes. In a stainless steel mixing bowl, combine Fig Balsamic Syrup with honey (if using) and set aside.

Place burrata in middle of square or rectangular plate and sprinkle with salt and pepper. Place 2 peach quarters and 2 shrimp on each side. Garnish cheese with microgreens. Drizzle perimeter of plate with Arbequina olive oil and honey-balsamic mixture and serve.

Worcestershire Vinaigrette
makes one quart

2½ Teaspoons Worcestershire sauce
2½ Teaspoons balsamic vinegar
½ Shallot, minced

½ Teaspoon minced garlic
2 Teaspoons water
¾ Cup extra-virgin olive oil

Add all ingredients except oil to a blender. Blend on medium speed until incorporated, then drizzle oil through spout until emulsified.

Bistro Steak Salad

Season steak with salt and pepper. On a hot grill, grill steak until medium rare, about 3½ minutes per side, and let rest for 2 minutes. Mix remaining ingredients in a small bowl. Add 2 tablespoons Worcestershire Vinaigrette and mix thoroughly. Nestle salad on one end of a large plate. When steak has rested, slice meat on the bias, for 6 slices total. Fan onto plate against the greens.

makes two servings

6	Ounces prime hanger steak
	Sea salt and black pepper
1	Handful wild arugula
1	Kumato tomato, quartered
1	Tablespoon crumbled Maytag blue cheese
1	Tablespoon Pickled Red Onion
	(recipe on page 90)
¼	Diced avocado
	Worcestershire Vinaigrette

Tarragon Vinaigrette
makes one cup

1 Tablespoon fresh tarragon
2 Tablespoons tarragon vinegar
1 Small shallot, minced
1 Small garlic clove, minced

1 Tablespoon crème fraîche
1 Cup extra-virgin olive oil
½ Teaspoon sea salt
¼ Teaspoon black pepper

Place all ingredients except for extra-virgin olive oil, salt, and pepper in a blender. Turn blender to medium speed and slowly add the extra-virgin olive oil. If the consistency is too thick, thin with small amounts of cold water. Season with salt and pepper. Extra dressing keeps in refrigerator for up to a week.

Ahi Tuna Niçoise

Heat oil in a sauté pan over high heat. Season tuna with salt and pepper. When oil starts to smoke, add the tuna; sear for no more than 35 seconds on each side. Remove from pan and cut each piece of tuna into 6 slices, length-wise.

Toss arugula with Tarragon Vinaigrette and spread across a serving plate. Arrange heirloom tomato, roasted red pepper, haricots verts, tuna, egg, onion, Niçoise olives, and potato in separate mounds atop the arugula, and season with a final sprinkle of salt and pepper.

makes two servings

2	Teaspoons extra-virgin olive oil
10	Ounces ahi tuna
	Sea salt and black pepper
4	Large handfuls arugula
2	Tablespoons Tarragon Vinaigrette
2	Heirloom cherry tomatoes, quartered
2	Large pieces roasted red pepper, sliced
16	Haricots verts, blanched
2	Hard-boiled eggs, sliced
12	Niçoise olives
2	Tablespoons red onion, shaved
2	Roasted fingerling potato, quartered

Mediterranean Salad

makes two servings

½	**Cup cooked farro**
6	**Tablespoons cooked red quinoa**
2	**Handfuls baby kale**
¼	**Cup shaved red onion**
12	**Heirloom cherry tomatoes, halved**
2	**Small Persian cucumbers, diced into ¼-inch cubes**
¼	**Cup crumbled feta**
16	**Kalamata olives**
½	**Teaspoon ground sumac**
¼	**Cup Lemon Vinaigrette**
	Sea salt

Place all ingredients except sumac and Lemon Vinaigrette into a serving bowl and mix thoroughly. Add Lemon Vinaigrette and sumac, season with salt, mix again, and serve.

Lemon Vinaigrette
Makes one cup

Juice of 2 lemons (about ½ cup)
1 teaspoon sea salt

¼ teaspoon black pepper
1 cup extra-virgin olive oil

In a medium bowl or jar, combine lemon juice, vinegar, salt, and pepper. Whisk, or cover and shake, until salt has dissolved. Add the extra-virgin olive oil and whisk or shake until thoroughly combined.

White Bean Salad

makes six servings

3	**5-ounce cans cannellini beans**
½	**Cup red onion, chopped**
½	**Cup fresh flat-leaf (Italian) parsley, chopped**
¼	**Cup fresh dill, mint, or basil, chopped**
	Sea salt and black pepper
	Lemon Vinaigrette, to taste
3	**Scallions, green part only, thinly sliced, for garnish**

Strain the beans and rinse with cool water. In a large mixing bowl, combine beans, onion, herbs, salt and pepper. Gently stir in Lemon Vinaigrette to taste. Transfer to a serving bowl and garnish with scallion greens.

makes four servings

¾	**Cup cucumber, peeled, seeded, and chopped**
½	**Vidalia onion, chopped**
½	**Cup yellow bell pepper, coarsely chopped**
3	**Tablespoons champagne vinegar**
½	**Tablespoon extra-virgin olive oil**
¼	**Teaspoon salt**
	Black pepper, to taste
1	**Pound (about 3 large) ripe yellow tomatoes, seeded and chopped**
1	**Small garlic clove, minced**
½	**Teaspoon of Arbequina Olive oil, for garnish**
2	**Teaspoons sliced basil leaves, for garnish**

Yellow Tomato Gazpacho

In a large bowl, combine all ingredients except for the Arbequina olive oil and basil. Place ⅓ of the mixture in a food processor or blender and puree until smooth; transfer to a large serving bowl. Repeat with the remaining mixture. Cover and chill until cold. Before serving, taste and adjust seasoning as needed, drizzle with Arbequina olive oil, and garnish with basil leaves.

Beet Salad

Preheat oven to 375°F. Place red and yellow beets in separate bowls. Drizzle each with 1 tablespoon of extra-virgin olive oil and season with salt and pepper. Add the champagne vinegar to the yellow beets and 1 tablespoon balsamic vinegar to the red beets; stir to coat. Wrap the yellow beets and red beets in 2 separate foil pouches, place on a baking pan, and roast for 45 to 50 minutes. Once cooked, remove from the foil pouches and let cool.

Slice the (raw) striped beet as thinly as possible, preferably using a mandoline, and let the slices rest in ice water. Use a paper towel to rub the skin off 4 of the red beets. Place in a blender with the remaining 1 tablespoon balsamic vinegar, 4 tablespoons extra-virgin olive oil, and 1 teaspoon cold water; puree on high until smooth. Peel 3 of the remaining red beets and dice. Peel the final 3 red beets and the 3 yellow beets and halve length-wise.

In a small bowl, combine the goat cheese, 4 tablespoons extra-virgin olive oil, salt, and pepper and use a fork to stir together until incorporated.

To plate the salad, place a quenelle of goat cheese in the center of the plate. Place the diced and the 2 colors of roasted beets in separate sections around it. Garnish each section with greens and slices of striped beet and decorate the plate with drizzles of beet puree.

makes two servings

10	**Red baby beets**
3	**Yellow baby beets**
10	**Tablespoons extra-virgin olive oil**
	Sea salt and black pepper
1	**Tablespoon champagne vinegar**
2	**Tablespoons balsamic vinegar, divided**
1	**Striped baby beet (optional)**
5	**Ounces goat cheese (preferably Laura Chenel)**
1	**Package microgreens or sprouts**

Maine Lobster Cobb Salad

Prepare the lobster: In a heavy stockpot, combine water, onion, chopped celery, bay leaves, parsley, lemon halves, and lemon juice and bring to a boil. Add lobster and boil for 7½ minutes. Meanwhile, prepare an ice bath. When cooked, remove lobster and place in ice bath for 4 minutes. Once cool, break apart claws and tail and extract meat.

In a mixing bowl, combine 5 ounces chopped lobster meat (save extra meat for another use) with the remaining ingredients, except the garnish. Toss gently to combine; taste and season with salt and pepper to taste. To serve, carefully arrange in a shallow bowl or entrée-size plate. Garnish with tarragon and lobster claw.

makes two servings

1	Medium onion, chopped
3	Stalks celery, chopped
2	Bay leaves
1	Bunch parsley
1	Lemon, halved and juiced, halves reserved
1	1½-pound live Maine lobster
2	Romaine hearts, chopped
2	Tablespoons chopped applewood-smoked bacon
2	Tablespoons crumbled Maytag blue cheese
8	Heirloom cherry tomatoes, halved
10	Green beans
2	Tablespoons chopped hard-boiled egg
1	Tablespoon chopped scallion
¼	Avocado, peeled and diced
4	Tablespoons Tarragon Vinaigrette *(recipe on page 63)*
	Sea salt and black pepper
1	Tarragon sprig, for garnish
1	Lobster claw, for garnish

makes six servings

1	Tablespoon extra-virgin olive oil
½	Medium yellow onion, diced
1	Medium tomato, diced
4	Garlic cloves, minced
¾	Pound ground beef chuck
1	Tablespoon chili powder
1	Tablespoon smoked paprika
¼	Teaspoon cayenne pepper
½	Teaspoon ground cumin
1	Bay leaf
	Sea salt and black pepper
4	Ounces tomato paste
16	Ounces chicken stock
½	Cup black beans
1	Cup kidney beans
	Shredded cheddar cheese, for garnish
	Sliced scallions, for garnish

Sirloin Chili

Warm extra-virgin olive oil in a large stockpot over medium heat. Add onions, tomato, and garlic and sauté until the onions become translucent—about 8 minutes. Add beef, spices, and bay leaves, season with salt and pepper, and sauté until beef is nearly cooked. Add tomato paste, chicken stock, and beans; bring to a low simmer and let cook for 3 minutes. Reduce heat to low and let cook, uncovered, for 1 hour. Taste and adjust seasoning as needed. Spoon into individual serving bowls and top with cheddar cheese and scallions.

Northern Halibut Filet

Salmon Burger

Baby New Zealand Lamb Chops

Pan-Seared Idaho Trout

Pan-Seared Salmon

Bucatini Limone

Braised Pork Butt

Snapper Soft Tacos

Maine Lobster Sliders

Warner Bros. Burger

Tuscan Chicken Sandwich

Braised Lamb Ragu

Smoked Salmon Pizza

Seared Rare Ahi Tuna

Branzino in Papillote

Wild Mushroom and Black Truffle Risotto

Chicken Paillard

Short Ribs

Squash Blossom Pizza

Gemelli Ragu

Smoked Salmon Tartine

Pizzetta Funghi

Seared Day Boat Scallops

MAIN DISHES

A main course at the commissary is an elegant affair. Historic deals have been brokered over pan-seared trout with potato-artichoke ragout, while creative revelations are shared across forkfuls of bucatini limone. On any given night, you'll find dishes for indulgent celebrations (mushroom and black truffle risotto, lamb chops with chermoula and smoked cheddar mac & cheese) alongside healthier bites, like chicken paillard topped with arugula salad and grilled snapper soft tacos with piquant salsa verde. Warner Bros. chefs cull inspiration from across the globe, ensuring a main event that's big on flavor, effortlessly sophisticated, and always satisfying.

Northern Halibut Filet

makes two servings

1	**Tablespoon sugar**
4	**Parsnips, peeled and chopped**
2	**Small russet potatoes, peeled and chopped**
8	**Tablespoons butter, softened, plus more for sautéing**
½	**Cup heavy cream**
	Sea salt and black pepper
3	**Baby zucchini, sliced on the bias**
3	**Figs, halved**
2	**Tablespoons extra-virgin olive oil**
2	**5½-ounce pieces Alaskan halibut filet**
1	**package microgreens, for garnish**
	Garlic flowers, for garnish, optional
	Fig Balsamic Syrup, for garnish

(recipe on page 52)

Boil the parsnips and potatoes in water until soft. Place through a food mill (or force through a fine-mesh strainer). Puree with butter and cream and season with salt and black pepper.

Heat a pat of butter in a separate sauté pan over medium heat and sauté zucchini and figs until tender. In another pan, heat extra-virgin olive oil over high until it begins to smoke; add halibut and sear for 2½ minutes per side. Remove from the heat and let rest in the pan for 1 minute.

To serve, spoon parsnip-potato puree onto plates and place halibut on top. Place 3 fig halves on the plate and tuck zucchini slices between. Drizzle balsamic-fig syrup across the plate, and garnish with microgreens and garlic flowers, if available.

Salmon Burgers

makes six burgers

2½	**Pounds fresh salmon, skin removed and roughly chopped**
3	**Shallots, minced**
1	**Tablespoon lemon zest**
1½	**Tablespoons fresh dill, chopped**
1	**Teaspoon sea salt**
1	**Tablespoon extra-virgin olive oil**
6	**Brioche buns, halved width-wise**
½	**Cup Tzatziki**
1	**Large heirloom tomato, cut into 6 slices**
1	**Avocado, sliced**
⅓	**Cup arugula**

In a large food processor, combine salmon, shallots, lemon zest, dill, and salt. Pulse for 2 seconds at a time, 6 or 7 times, until the mixture resembles ground burger meat, and all of the ingredients are incorporated. Use a spatula to transfer the mixture to a bowl. Divide into 6 portions and shape into patties. Place on a foil-lined roasting pan and refrigerate for 45 minutes to help firm the patties.

Heat extra-virgin olive oil in a large sauté pan over medium-high. Add the salmon burgers and cook for 3 to 4 minutes each side, until outside is browned and the center is just cooked through.

To serve, spread Tzatziki on warm brioche buns, add the salmon burgers, and top with heirloom tomato, avocado, and arugula.

Tzatziki
makes one cup

½ Persian cucumber, peeled and seeded
1 4-ounce container plain Greek yogurt
1 4-ounce container labne (Middle Eastern strained yogurt)
1 Tablespoon extra-virgin olive oil

Zest and juice of ½ small lemon
½ Tablespoon fresh dill, chopped
2 Cloves garlic, minced

Using a mandoline or very sharp knife, halve the cucumber and slice into paper-thin discs. In a mixing bowl, combine cucumber with the remaining ingredients and season with salt and pepper. Stir well to combine, taste, and season as needed. Let rest in the refrigerator for at least 1 hour before serving.

Baby New Zealand Lamb Chops with Mac & Cheese

Preheat oven to 375°F. In a large bowl, combine pasta and Cheese Sauce and stir well to combine. Portion Mac & Cheese into 4 individual cast-iron dishes or 1 large baking dish, sprinkle reserved grated cheese on top, and bake for 8 minutes.

Brush lamb chops with extra-virgin olive oil and season with salt and black pepper. Grill over high heat for 3 minutes per side, until medium-rare. Let rest for 3 minutes before serving. Serve with Mac & Cheese and Chermoula on the side.

makes four servings

1	**1-pound box orecchiette pasta, cooked**
2	**Cups Cheese Sauce,**
	plus reserved grated cheese
12	**Baby lamb chops**
	Sea salt and black pepper
½	**Cup Chermoula**
¼	**Cup extra-virgin olive oil**

Cheese Sauce
makes two cups

1 Cup whole milk
1 Cup heavy cream
1 Teaspoon minced garlic
⅓ Cup roughly grated smoked cheddar cheese

½ Cup roughly grated Parmesan cheese
⅓ Cup roughly grated Vermont white cheddar cheese
½ Teaspoon smoked sea salt
⅛ Teaspoon black pepper

In a 4-quart saucepot (preferably nonstick) over medium heat, bring the milk, cream, and garlic to a simmer, being careful not to scald the milk. Once simmering, lower the heat to medium-low and add the cheese, a handful at a time, whisking constantly or blending with an immersion blender. (Reserve some of the cheese for baking.) When finished, the mixture should be silky and thick. Add salt and pepper and stir once more.

Chermoula
makes approximately one cup

¼ Teaspoon coriander seeds
6 Whole black peppercorns
⅛ Teaspoon dried red pepper flakes
Small pinch saffron threads, crumbled
¼ Teaspoon sea salt
½ Teaspoon paprika

½ Medium onion, minced (about 1 cup)
2½ Tablespoons finely chopped fresh parsley leaves
¼ Cup finely chopped cilantro leaves
1 Tablespoon lemon zest
Juice of ½ lemon
1 Cup extra-virgin olive oil
2 Large garlic cloves, minced

With a mortar and pestle, electric spice grinder, or cleaned coffee grinder, finely grind the coriander seeds, peppercorns, red pepper flakes, and saffron. Transfer the spice mixture to a blender or food processor, add the remaining ingredients and puree until smooth, adding water a tablespoon at a time, as needed. Keep refrigerated, in a covered container, for up to 2 weeks.

Pan-Seared Idaho Trout

makes two servings

2	**Whole, head-on Idaho trout, cleaned and partially deboned**
	Sea salt and black pepper
1	**Cup plus 3 tablespoons extra-virgin olive oil**
11	**Garlic cloves, 10 whole and 1 minced**
2	**Bay leaves**
10	**Fingerling potatoes**
1	**8-ounce jar grilled artichokes in oil**
12	**Heirloom cherry tomatoes**
1	**Tablespoon flat-leaf (Italian) parsley, chopped**
2	**Tablespoons pine nuts, toasted**
2	**Tablespoons butter**
1	**Lemon wedge**

Season fish with salt and black pepper, on both sides and inside, and set aside. In a small pot over medium heat, bring 1 cup extra-virgin olive oil to a simmer; add 10 garlic cloves, bay leaves, and potatoes. Poach potatoes and garlic until soft in the center (use a toothpick to check). Once soft, remove from the heat and let cool.

Warm 2 tablespoons extra-virgin olive oil in a sauté pan over medium-high heat; add artichokes, heirloom tomatoes, and minced garlic and stir. Add roasted garlic and potatoes; sauté for 2 minutes, stir in parsley and pine nuts, and remove from the heat.

Heat the remaining tablespoon of extra-virgin olive oil in a large pan over high heat. Sauté trout until flesh is opaque and soft—about 2 minutes per side. Remove trout from pan and place on serving plates. Return vegetables to the heat, add butter, and stir until butter is melted and vegetables are coated. Squeeze lemon over vegetables, stir to combine, and spoon mixture over top of the fish.

Pan-Seared Salmon

makes two servings

12	**Peewee potatoes**
1½	**Cups plus 4 teaspoons extra-virgin olive oil**
2	**Bay leaves**
2	**Rosemary sprigs**
4	**Garlic cloves**
3	**Ounces slab bacon, cut into ¼-inch pieces**
2	**6-ounce pieces skin-on Atlantic salmon**
	Sea salt and black pepper
4	**Handfuls baby kale**
½	**Cup vegetable stock**
2	**Tablespoons unsalted butter**
2	**Lemon wedges**
2	**Teaspoons chopped parsley**

In a small pot, combine potatoes, ¾ cup extra-virgin olive oil, bay leaf, rosemary, and garlic. Bring to a simmer and cook until potatoes are easily pierced with a toothpick—about 30 minutes. Remove potatoes from oil; let cool and cut in half. Place bacon in a sauté pan over low heat and let render slowly. Bacon is ready once 75 percent of its fat has rendered out.

Season salmon with salt and pepper. Heat 2 teaspoons extra-virgin olive oil in a sauté pan over high heat. When oil begins to smoke, place fish into pan, skin side down, and cook until skin is crisp—about 2½ minutes. Flip fish, reduce heat to medium, cook for 2½ minutes more, and turn off heat. Leave salmon in pan over warm burner while you cook the vegetables.

In a separate sauté pan over high heat, add 2 teaspoons extra-virgin olive oil, bacon, potatoes, and kale; stir until kale begins to wilt. Add vegetable stock and stir. Immediately remove kale from pan and set in the center of a serving plate. Add butter to pan and squeeze lemon wedge over top. Stir well and let cook until liquid in pan is reduced and thick enough to coat a spoon. To serve, place potatoes and bacon over the kale and set salmon on top. Stir parsley into the pan juices and drizzle sauce across the plate to serve.

Bucatini Limone

Bring a large pot of water to a boil, salt heavily, and cook the pasta for 10 to 12 minutes until al dente. Strain, run under cold water to stop the cooking process, and set aside. In a small pot over medium heat, bring the extra-virgin olive oil to a light simmer. Add the lemon slices and cook until golden brown. Remove with a slotted spoon and set aside.

In a large sauté pan over medium-high heat, heat the remaining teaspoon of extra-virgin olive oil. Add garlic and sauté for a few seconds, then add pasta and toss well to coat. Add lemon juice and butter and toss to coat; add spinach and toss again. Once the spinach is lightly wilted, add lemon slices and 4 tablespoons of Parmesan, season with salt, toss well, and turn into serving bowls. Garnish with parsley, the remaining tablespoon of cheese, and lemon slices.

makes four servings

1	1-pound package Bucatini pasta
3	Cups plus 1 teaspoon extra-virgin olive oil
1	Whole lemon, thinly sliced
1	Teaspoon garlic, chopped
	Juice of 1 large lemon
2	Tablespoons butter
4	Packed cups fresh spinach
5	Tablespoons finely grated Parmesan cheese
	Sea salt
1	Tablespoon flat-leaf (Italian) parsley, chopped

Braised Pork Butt

Preheat oven to 275°F. Rub pork butt with 3 tablespoons oil and season liberally with salt and pepper. In a large Dutch oven over medium-high heat, place meat fat-side down; brown each side for about 5 minutes. Remove meat from pot and pour off most of the remaining fat, reserving enough to sauté the aromatics. Add celery, onions, and garlic and sauté until translucent—about 5 minutes. Add tomato and deglaze the pot with apple cider vinegar and whiskey. Add beer and return meat to pot. Bring to a simmer over high heat and cover. Transfer to oven and roast for 3 hours.

After 3 hours, remove pot from oven and skim off excess fat. Add potato, turnip, celeriac, parsnips, carrots, and granulated sugar and cover. Return to oven for 45 minutes. When finished cooking, the meat and vegetables should be fork-tender. Remove the meat and vegetables and keep warm.

Bring a large pot of water to a boil and cook the sweet potatoes until soft. Transfer to a blender and puree with butter and brown sugar.

Heat remaining 1 tablespoon oil in a sauté pan over medium. Add shallot, sauté until soft, and add cavolo nero. Sauté for 2 minutes, then deglaze pan with a spoonful of pork-whiskey jus. Remove from heat once kale is wilted and season with salt and pepper.

To serve, slice meat across the grain in 3-inch by 3-inch chunks. Place a large spoonful of sweet potato puree on the plate and top with cavolo nero and the braised pork and vegetables. Spoon 4 tablespoons of pork-whiskey jus over top and garnish with Red Onion Marmalade.

makes six servings

1	Boneless Boston pork butt (5 pounds)
4	Tablespoons extra-virgin olive oil
	Sea salt and black pepper
2	Stalks celery, diced
2	Medium onions, diced
8	Cloves garlic, minced
1	Plum tomato, diced
½	Cup apple cider vinegar
4	Ounces Jameson whiskey
4	12-ounce bottles IPA beer
1	Baking or Idaho potato, peeled and cut into 1-inch cubes
1	Turnip, peeled and cut into 1-inch cubes
1	Celeriac, peeled and diced
2	Parsnips, peeled and diced
2	Carrots, peeled and diced
½	Cup granulated sugar
4	Sweet potatoes, peeled and cut into 1-inch cubes
6	Tablespoons butter
½	Cup brown sugar
1	Large shallot, thinly sliced
1	Bunch cavolo nero (black kale), stems removed, leaves roughly chopped
	Red Onion Marmalade, for garnish

(recipe on page 86)

Red Onion Marmalade
Makes approximately one cup

2 Tablespoons extra-virgin olive oil
1 Tablespoon butter
2 Large red onions, thinly sliced
¼ Cup granulated sugar

1 Cup red wine (preferably Merlot)
¼ Cup balsamic vinegar
Sea salt and black pepper

Heat oil and butter in a large skillet over medium; add onions and sugar and sauté until onions start to caramelize—about 15 minutes. Add red wine and balsamic vinegar, stir well, and bring to a boil. Reduce heat to medium-low and simmer until liquid is evaporated—about 15 to 20 minutes. Season with salt and pepper.

Snapper Soft Tacos

makes two servings (two tacos each)

7	**Ounces red snapper**
1	**Teaspoon extra-virgin olive oil**
	Sea salt and black pepper
4	**6-inch white corn tortillas**
2	**Tablespoons queso fresco, diced or crumbled**
1	**Handful purple and green cabbage, shredded**
½	**Cup Pico de Gallo**
	Salsa Verde

Pre-heat grill. Coat fish with oil and season well with salt and pepper. Once grill is hot, cook fish for 3 to 4 minutes. Warm tortillas on the grill—about 20 seconds each side. In a mixing bowl, combine cheese, cabbage, and Pico de Gallo. Place fish in tortillas, top with Pico de Gallo, and serve with Salsa Verde on the side.

Pico de Gallo
makes one cup

3 Roma tomatoes, diced
½ Small red onion, diced
⅛ Bunch cilantro, chopped

½ Jalapeño, seeded and finely diced
Juice of ½ small lemon
Sea salt and black pepper, to taste

Place all ingredients in a stainless steel mixing bowl and stir about 1 minute. Season with salt and pepper to taste. Let stand at room temperature 30 to 40 minutes before serving.

Salsa Verde
makes one cup

4 Large tomatillos, halved
½ Spanish onion, chopped
1 Jalapeño, halved and seeded
2 Garlic cloves, smashed and chopped
Olive oil

⅛ Cup cold water
½ Avocado, chopped
Juice of ½ lime
½ Bunch cilantro
Sea salt and pepper

Preheat oven to 350°F. Place tomatillos, onion, jalapeños, and garlic on a sheet tray and drizzle with oil. Bake for 25 to 30 minutes. Remove and let cool. Once cooled, place the roasted vegetables in a blender and puree. Add water, avocado, and lime juice and puree for 1 minute; add cilantro and puree for 2 minutes. Season with salt and pepper as needed.

To Cook the Lobster

8 Quarts water	1 Bunch parsley
1 Medium onion, chopped	1 Lemon, halved and juiced,
3 Stalks celery, chopped	halves reserved
2 Bay leaves	1 1½-pound live Maine lobster

To Prepare the Sliders

3 Brioche buns,	3 Heirloom cherry
halved width-wise	tomatoes
Butter	Knotted toothpicks
Lobster Salad	Sea salt kettle chips
12 Arugula leaves	

Maine Lobster Sliders

Prepare the lobster: In a heavy stockpot, combine water, onion, chopped celery, bay leaves, parsley, lemon halves, and lemon juice and bring to a boil. Add lobster and boil for 7½ minutes. Meanwhile, prepare an ice bath. When cooked, remove lobster and place in ice bath for 4 minutes. Once cool, break apart claws and tail and extract meat.

Make the lobster salad: In a large bowl, combine lobster with diced celery, onion, shallot, tarragon, tarragon vinegar, lemon, mayonnaise, and crème fraîche. Mix well and season with salt and pepper to taste.

To assemble the sliders, butter and grill the brioche buns. On the bottom of each bun, spoon ¼ cup plus 1 tablespoon of the lobster salad. Add 4 arugula leaves and top with half of the bun. To hold sandwich together, place 1 heirloom tomato on a knotted toothpick, then place through the center of bun. Serve with sea salt kettle chips.

Lobster Salad

makes three sliders

	Lobster meat, chopped
2	Stalks celery, diced
½	Red onion, diced
1	Small shallot, diced
2	Tablespoons chopped fresh tarragon
1	Teaspoon tarragon vinegar
	Zest and juice of 1 lemon
¼	Cup mayonnaise
2	Tablespoons crème fraîche
	Sea salt and black pepper, to taste

Warner Bros. Burger

Separate and weigh the meat to make 2 8-ounce burger patties. Season with salt, pepper, and garlic salt. Grill the patties for 3 minutes per side until cooked to medium. Place on warm brioche buns and top with lettuce, tomato, and onion. Serve with ketchup and mustard on the side.

makes two to four burgers

1	Pound ground beef (Warner Bros.' signature blend is 50% ground Angus sirloin, 30% ground brisket, 20% fat)
	Sea salt and black pepper
	Garlic salt
2	Brioche burger buns, warmed
4	Bibb lettuce leaves
6	Thin slices tomato
2	Thin slices sweet onion

Tuscan Chicken Sandwich

makes two servings

2	**Teaspoons extra-virgin olive oil**
2	**6-ounce chicken breasts, seasoned with salt and pepper**
2	**Slices provolone cheese**
2	**Teaspoons Basil Aioli**
2	**Artisan bread rolls, warmed**
6	**Tablespoons Pickled Red Onion**
2	**Small handfuls arugula**
2	**Large pieces roasted red pepper**
6	**Slices tomato**

Heat extra-virgin olive oil in a sauté pan over medium-high. Add the chicken breast and cook for 2 minutes on one side; flip, lower the heat to medium, and cook until cooked through. About 1 minute before chicken is done, place cheese on top and cover the pan to melt the cheese. Spread Basil Aioli on the top half of the bun and place the chicken on the bottom. Top the chicken with pickled onion, roasted pepper, tomato, arugula, and the top half of the bun.

Basil Aioli
makes one cup

8 Basil leaves
Bunch flat-leaf (Italian) parsley
2 Cloves minced garlic
Juice of 1 small lemon
2 Tablespoons cold water

1 Egg yolk
½ Cup extra-virgin olive oil
½ Cup mayonnaise
Sea salt and black pepper

Bring a small pot of water to boil and prepare an ice bath. Blanch the basil and parsley leaves for no more than 10 seconds; quickly remove from the boiling water and plunge into the ice bath. Once cool, place in a blender with garlic, lemon juice, cold water, and egg yolk. Start the blender on a low speed and slowly increase to high. Add extra-virgin olive oil in a steady drizzle; the mixture should begin to thicken and turn a pale green. After the extra-virgin olive oil is incorporated, add mayonnaise and blend a few seconds more until fully incorporated. Season with salt and pepper.

Pickled Red Onion
Makes one cup

⅛ Cup cold water
1 Teaspoon kosher salt
1 Tablespoon granulated sugar
3 Black peppercorns

1 Red onion, thinly sliced
⅓ Cup apple cider vinegar
1 Bay leaf

In a stainless steel mixing bowl, combine water, salt, sugar, and peppercorns; stir and let sit for 2 minutes or until sugar and salt are dissolved. In a separate mixing bowl, combine red onion, vinegar, and bay leaf and let stand for 30 minutes. Combine the 2 mixtures and refrigerate, covered, for at least 1 full day before use.

Braised Lamb Ragu

Season lamb shanks with salt and pepper. In a large braising pan, warm 2 tablespoons extra-virgin olive oil over high heat. Add lamb and brown on all sides—about 8 minutes. Remove lamb from pan, discard fat, and reduce heat to medium. Add 1 tablespoon extra-virgin olive oil, onion, garlic, chiles, bay leaves, and celery. Cook, stirring often, until onion is tender and begins to caramelize—about 8 minutes. Place tomatoes in a blender with ½ cup water and pulse 5 times to coarsely blend. Return lamb to pan with vegetables. Add tomatoes, stock, and wine and cover (with a lid or aluminum foil). Place pan over medium-high heat for 10 minutes, then reduce heat to low and cook for 1½ hours. Once done, transfer lamb to a sheet pan; when cool enough to handle, pull meat from the bone in chunks, discarding fat and sinew. Return lamb meat and bones to pan and simmer over low heat until sauce thickens and reduces by half. Remove bones and season with salt and pepper to taste.

Bring a pot of salted water to a boil and cook pappardelle according to package instructions, until al dente. In the interim, heat remaining 1 tablespoon extra-virgin olive oil in a large pan over high heat and sauté mushrooms and peas for 2 minutes. Add 4 cups lamb ragu, stir to combine, and cook for 2 minutes more. Add pasta, toss well to coat, and transfer to 6 serving bowls. Serve topped with grated Parmesan cheese.

makes six servings

2	**1¼-pound lamb shanks (volcano cut)**
1	**1-pound package pappardelle**
	Sea salt and black pepper, to taste
4	**Tablespoons extra-virgin olive oil**
1	**Yellow onion, finely chopped**
6	**Garlic cloves, minced**
2	**Calabrian chiles, finely chopped**
2	**Bay leaves**
3	**Celery stalks, finely chopped**
4	**Large tomatoes, roughly chopped**
24	**Ounces chicken stock**
12	**Ounces red wine (preferably Italian, like Sangiovese or Nebbiolo)**
1	**Cup hedgehog or chanterelle mushrooms (halved, if large)**
1	**Cup spring peas (fresh or frozen)**
	Grated Parmesan cheese, for serving

Smoked Salmon Pizza

Preheat oven to 450°F. Roll the Pizza Dough into a 10- or 12-inch round and place on an oiled baking sheet. Bake for 7 to 8 minutes, then remove and let cool slightly. Spread with crème fraîche, leaving 1 inch around the edges. Top with salmon, onion, and capers. Mix arugula with Citrus Vinaigrette and place atop pizza. Brush crust with Chile Oil and serve.

makes one individual pizza

1	**Ball Pizza Dough** *(recipe on page 106)*
3	**Tablespoons Dill Crème Fraîche** *(recipe on page 104)*
4½	**Ounces smoked salmon**
½	**Tablespoon red onion, shaved**
1	**Teaspoon capers**
½	**Cup arugula**
½	**Teaspoon Citrus Vinaigrette** *(recipe on page 97)*
	Chile Oil *(recipe on page 93)*

Chile Oil
makes approximately one cup

1 Cup extra-virgin olive oil
2 Teaspoons dried crushed red pepper flakes

½ Teaspoon paprika

Combine the extra-virgin olive oil, crushed red pepper flakes, and paprika in a heavy small saucepan. Cook over low heat until a thermometer inserted into the oil registers 180°F, about 5 minutes. Remove from heat. Cool to room temperature, about 2 hours. Transfer the oil and pepper flakes to a bottle. Seal the lid. Refrigerate up to 1 month.

Seared Rare Ahi Tuna

makes two servings

2	Ears corn, shucked
1	Red bell pepper
16	Yellow wax beans
16	Green beans
20	Pods edamame
1	Shallot, minced
1	Teaspoon garlic, minced
10	Heirloom cherry tomatoes, minced
2	Sprigs fresh oregano or marjoram
2	5-ounce pieces ahi tuna (brick cut)
	Sea salt and black pepper
2	Teaspoons extra-virgin olive oil, divided
¼	Cup butter
¾	Cup chicken stock

On a hot grill, cook the corn until slightly charred and the red pepper until fully charred. Cut the kernels from the corn cob and place in a mixing bowl. Place the charred pepper in a paper bag to sweat for 15 minutes. Run under cool water to remove the charred skin. Slice and seed the pepper, then mince and add to the bowl with the corn.

Prepare a pot of boiling salted water and an ice bath. Blanch wax and green beans simultaneously for 35 seconds, then remove and shock in the ice bath. Add to the bowl with the corn and pepper. In the same pot, blanch edamame for 2 minutes then shock in the ice bath. Remove beans from pods and add to the mixing bowl, along with the shallot, garlic, and heirloom tomatoes. Pick the leaves from oregano/marjoram, discard the stems, and reserve leaves in a small bowl.

Season the tuna with salt and pepper. Heat 1 teaspoon of extra-virgin olive oil in a sauté pan over high heat. Add the ingredients from the mixing bowl and stir steadily for about 1 minute. Add the butter and sauté for another minute, stirring regularly so the vegetables don't burn. Add chicken stock and oregano/marjoram, reserving a few leaves for garnish. Lower the heat and simmer until stock is reduced by half—about 5 minutes.

Heat the remaining teaspoon of extra-virgin olive oil in a sauté pan over high heat. When oil starts to smoke, add the tuna steaks; sear for no more than 35 seconds on each side. Remove from pan and cut length-wise. Place a spoonful of vegetables at the center of each plate, top with tuna, and garnish with the remaining oregano/marjoram.

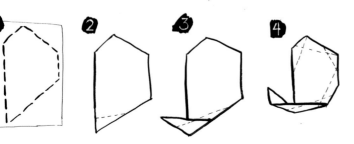

Branzino in Papillote

makes two servings

2	Teaspoons extra-virgin olive oil
8	Baby zucchini, thinly sliced Purple
8	peewee potatoes, blanched, chilled, and halved
2	Small fennel bulbs, thinly sliced
2	Garlic cloves, minced
1	Shallot, sliced
2	5-ounce branzino filets, seasoned with salt and black pepper
1	Tablespoon butter
1	Teaspoon plus 2 small sprigs thyme
2	Sprigs rosemary
2	Sheets parchment paper

Preheat oven to 400°F. Heat extra-virgin olive oil in a pan over medium heat; add zucchini, potatoes, fennel, garlic, and shallot, sauté for about 2 minutes and then remove from the heat and let cool. Rest parchment paper on a baking dish. Place vegetable mixture in center of the parchment paper, including any juices released from the vegetables while cooking. Place the branzino, butter, thyme, and rosemary atop the vegetables and fold the parchment over the fish. Starting at one corner, begin folding and tucking the edges to form a pouch. Work your way around, keeping it tight. At the end, tuck the end under the pouch and use a safety pin to secure it. Bake for 12 to 14 minutes, until pouch fully puffs up. Tear open and serve.

Wild Mushroom and Black Truffle Risotto

Bring broth to simmer in a 4-quart saucepot. Reduce heat to low and cover to keep hot. In a separate 4-quart pot over medium heat, melt butter and extra-virgin olive oil. Add shallots and sauté for 1 minute; add mushrooms and sauté until tender and juices are released—about 8 minutes. Add rice and stir to coat.

Add wine and simmer until liquid is absorbed, stirring frequently—about 8 minutes. Increase heat to medium-high; add ¾ cup hot chicken broth and simmer until absorbed, stirring frequently. Add the remaining broth, ¾ cup at a time, stirring frequently and allowing broth to be absorbed before adding more. Continue until rice is just tender and the mixture is creamy—about 20 minutes (note: you may not need to use all the broth).

Stir in Parmesan and thyme, taste, and season with salt to taste. Fold in black truffles and serve with more Parmesan sprinkled on top.

makes four servings

5½	**Cups chicken broth**
3	**Tablespoons butter**
3	**Tablespoons extra-virgin olive oil**
2	**Shallots, finely chopped**
1	**Pound mixed mushrooms (oyster, crimini, chanterelle), sliced**
1	**Cup arborio rice, uncooked**
½	**Cup dry white wine**
½	**Cup finely grated Parmesan cheese**
½	**Teaspoon fresh thyme, chopped**
	Sea salt, to taste
3	**Tablespoons black truffle shavings in truffle oil**

Chicken Paillard

Line a cutting board with plastic wrap, place the chicken breast on top, and fold one edge of the plastic wrap over the chicken. Use a mallet or a small, heavy pan to pound the chicken until it's ¼-inch thick. Remove from the plastic and set on a baking tray. Brush both sides of the chicken with 1 tablespoon Citrus Vinaigrette and let marinate for 30 minutes. Boil a pot of salted water and blanch the beans for 35 seconds. Shock in an ice bath to stop cooking, and then remove. Add shaved onion to ice bath for 20 minutes to remove any bitterness.

Heat a grill and season the chicken with salt and pepper. Grill chicken for 1½ minutes, then turn clockwise 1 quarter-turn. (Because it is so thin, the chicken does not need to be flipped while cooking.) Watch the chicken closely; as soon as the top is opaque, it is done. Turn off heat and flip chicken in pan.

In a mixing bowl, toss beans, onion, heirloom tomatoes, olives, and arugula with 2 tablespoons Citrus Vinaigrette, and season with salt and black pepper. Place the chicken on a plate and heap the salad over ¾ of it, leaving part exposed to show off its nice grill marks.

makes two servings

2	**6-ounce free-range chicken breasts**
6	**Tablespoons Citrus Vinaigrette** *(recipe on page 97)*
16	**Haricots verts**
16	**Yellow wax beans**
4	**Tablespoons red onion, shaved**
10	**Heirloom cherry tomatoes, halved**
16	**Niçoise olives**
4	**Large handfuls arugula**

Citrus Vinaigrette
makes one cup

½ Shallot, finely chopped
½ Cup extra-virgin olive oil
2 Tablespoons champagne vinegar

Juice of 1 lemon wedge
1 Tablespoon orange juice
¼ Teaspoon lemon zest
Sea salt and black pepper

Place all ingredients into a blender and mix on medium speed for 1½ minutes until emulsified. Let rest overnight, to let flavors marry, and shake well before using.

Short Ribs

Preheat oven to 325°F. Season short ribs with salt and pepper. Heat oil in a large Dutch oven over medium-high. Working in 2 batches, brown short ribs on all sides—about 8 minutes per batch. Transfer short ribs to a plate. Pour off all but 3 tablespoons of drippings from pot.

Add onions, carrots, and celery to pot and cook over medium-high heat, stirring often, until onions are browned—about 5 minutes. Add flour and tomato paste; cook, stirring constantly, until well combined and deep red—2 to 3 minutes. Stir in wine and add short ribs with any accumulated juices. Bring to a boil; lower heat to medium and simmer until wine is reduced by half—about 25 minutes. Add all herbs to pot along with garlic. Stir in stock. Bring to a boil, cover, and transfer to oven.

Cook until short ribs are tender—about 2½ to 3 hours. Transfer short ribs to a platter. Strain sauce from pot into a measuring cup. Spoon fat from surface of sauce and discard; season sauce to taste with salt and pepper. Serve short ribs in shallow bowls over White Cheddar Grits and Tiny Vegetables, with sauce spooned over top.

makes six servings

3¼	**Pounds boneless beef short ribs (preferably Niman Ranch country short rib)**
	Sea salt and black pepper
3	**Tablespoons extra-virgin olive oil**
3	**Medium onions, peeled and chopped**
3	**Medium carrots, peeled and chopped**
2	**Celery stalks, chopped**
3	**Tablespoons all-purpose flour**
1	**Tablespoon tomato paste**
1	**750 ml bottle red wine (preferably Cabernet Sauvignon)**
10	**Sprigs flat-leaf (Italian) parsley**
8	**Sprigs thyme**
4	**Sprigs oregano**
2	**Sprigs rosemary**
2	**Fresh or dried bay leaves**
1	**Head of garlic, halved crosswise**
4	**Cups low-sodium beef stock**
	White Cheddar Grits
	Tiny Vegetables

White Cheddar Grits
makes six servings

5 Cups water, plus more if needed
1½ Cups white Anson Mills grits (do not use instant)
4 Tablespoons butter

3 Ounces sharp Vermont white cheddar cheese
1½ Teaspoons sea salt
¼ Teaspoon smoked paprika

Bring water to a boil in a medium pot. Slowly add grits to water, whisking constantly, and cook until mixture starts to thicken—about 2 minutes. Reduce heat to medium-low and add butter; simmer gently, stirring occasionally, until grits are smooth, thick, and fall easily from the spoon—about 20 to 25 minutes. Add cheese, salt, and smoked paprika and stir just until cheese melts. Serve immediately, or cover and keep grits warm over low heat, stirring occasionally, for up to 1 hour (if opting for this, you may need to adjust the consistency with additional water just before serving).

Tiny Vegetables
makes six servings

Assortment of baby/small vegetables from the farmer's market

Butter
Sea salt and black pepper

Clean vegetables with a kitchen towel and cut any stalks down to 1 inch. Blanch in boiling water until just tender (about 45 seconds), strain, and let cool. To warm for serving, heat a pat of butter in a sauté pan over medium-low heat and gently sauté the vegetables until warm—about 2 minutes. Season with salt and pepper.

Basil Pesto
makes about one cup

2½ Cups packed basil leaves
3 Cloves garlic
½ Cup Parmesan cheese, grated

½ Cup extra-virgin olive oil
2 Tablespoons pine nuts
Sea salt and black pepper

Place all ingredients into a food processor. Pulse several times and then mix on high for about 40 seconds until smooth and incorporated. Season with salt and pepper to taste.

Squash Blossom Pizza

Preheat oven to 450°F. Roll the Pizza Dough into a 10- or 12-inch round, place on an oiled baking sheet, and bake until 75% cooked—about 5 minutes. Spread Basil Pesto across the dough, leaving 1 inch around the edges. Top with tomato slices and zucchini. In a small bowl, sprinkle squash blossoms with oil, salt, and pepper and mix. Place the squash blossoms and the burrata on the pizza. Return pizza to oven and bake for 5 minutes more, or until cheese is bubbling and edges are browned. Remove, brush crust with Chile Oil, and serve.

makes one individual pizza

1	**Ball Pizza Dough** *(recipe on page 106)*
2½	**Tablespoons Basil Pesto**
1	**Medium tomato, cut into 5 slices**
4	**Baby zucchini, sliced paper-thin**
5	**Squash blossoms**
	Extra-virgin olive oil
	Sea salt and black pepper
5	**Tablespoons burrata**
	Chile Oil *(recipe on page 93)*

Gemelli Ragu

makes four servings

1	**1-pound box Gemelli pasta**
½	**Head radicchio, quartered**
	Extra-virgin olive oil
	Sea salt and black pepper
2½	**Cups Pork Ragu**
½	**Cup warm chicken stock or pasta cooking water**
1	**Tablespoon Calabrian chiles, chopped**
5	**Tablespoons Parmesan cheese, finely grated, for garnish**

Bring a large pot of water to a rolling boil and salt it heavily. Add the pasta, stir gently, and let return to a boil. Let pasta cook uncovered, stirring occasionally, for 12 minutes, then drain (reserving cooking water, if using). While the pasta is cooking, brush the radicchio with extra-virgin olive oil, season with salt and pepper, and grill (or sear in a hot pan) until slightly charred.

Heat the Pork Ragu in a large sauté pan over medium-high heat. Add pasta and chicken stock or cooking water and stir well to combine. Let the sauce simmer, tossing frequently, for 1 to 2 minutes, then add radicchio and Calabrian chiles and stir well. Transfer to 4 serving bowls and garnish with Parmesan cheese.

Pork Ragu
makes two and a half cups

½ Tablespoon extra-virgin olive oil
½ Large Spanish onion, diced
1 Large carrot, diced
1 Large stalk celery, diced
1 Pound ground pork
½ Pound ground Italian sausage
Kosher salt and black pepper
1 Teaspoon dried oregano
4 Garlic cloves, smashed and roughly chopped

1 Cup tomato paste
1½ Cups hearty red wine, like Nebbiolo or Syrah
1½ Cups Marinara Sauce
½ Cup water
1 Bay leaf
1 Sprig of rosemary, leaves removed and chopped
1 Bunch thyme, tied in a bundle

Heat extra-virgin olive oil in a large saucepan over medium-high. Add onion, carrot, and celery and sauté, stirring frequently, until nicely browned—about 10 to 15 minutes. Add ground pork and Italian sausage, season with salt and pepper and stir to combine. Add dried oregano and garlic, stir, and continue to cook, stirring occasionally, until the meat is thoroughly browned—another 12 to 15 minutes.

Add tomato paste, stir well and cook 5 minutes more. Add red wine and simmer until reduced by half—another 5 minutes. Add marinara sauce, water, bay leaves, rosemary, and thyme, and stir well to combine. Turn up heat and bring sauce to a boil, then lower heat and let simmer, stirring occasionally, for 1½ hours. Add water as needed, 2 cups at a time, to prevent sauce from sticking. When finished, the sauce should be thick and hearty. Taste for seasoning; add salt and pepper as needed.

Marinara Sauce
makes two quarts

2 Tablespoons extra-virgin olive oil
5 Ounces diced Spanish onions
⅓ Cup diced carrots
⅓ Cup diced celery
1 Teaspoon chopped fresh thyme
1½ Teaspoons dried oregano
½ Cup minced garlic

2½ Pounds chopped fresh Roma tomatoes, chopped
1½ Large cans (1 pounds 10 ounces total) of crushed unpeeled tomatoes
1 Quart water
½ Cup sugar
1 Tablespoon kosher salt
½ Tablespoon black pepper
1½ Teaspoons chopped basil

Heat extra-virgin olive oil in a large saucepot over medium-high heat. Add onions, carrots, and celery and sauté until the onions are translucent—about 10 minutes. Add thyme, oregano, and garlic and sauté 5 minutes more. Add Roma tomatoes, lower the heat to medium, sauté for 5 minutes, and then add canned tomatoes, water, sugar, salt, and pepper. Let simmer for 1 hour, then let cool. Once cool, add fresh basil and, in a large blender or food processor, puree the sauce. Use the sauce within 1 week, or freeze.

2 ½-inch Thick slices Pullman olive bread, or a similar light, loaf-style bread
1 Radish (preferably French breakfast)
2 Tablespoons Dill Crème Fraîche

4 Ounces smoked salmon
3 Tablespoons Pickled Red Onion *(recipe on page 90)*
1 Teaspoon capers
1 Teaspoon Arbequina olive oil
1 Handful arugula

Dill Crème Fraîche
¾ Cup crème fraîche
1 Tablespoon dill, chopped
½ Shallot, minced
Juice of 1 lemon wedge
Sea salt and black pepper

Smoked Salmon Tartine
makes two servings

Toast the bread, cut each slice in half diagonally, and spread with Dill Crème Fraîche. Slice radish paper-thin, either on a mandoline or with a very sharp knife, and let sit in cold water for 2 minutes. Place smoked salmon on the bread, sprinkle with Pickled Red Onion and capers, and drizzle with extra-virgin olive oil. Garnish with arugula and radish slices.

Dill Creme Fraiche: In a small bowl, combine the ingredients and mix well.

Pizzetta Funghi

makes one pizza

Preheat oven to 425°F. Dust a hard surface with flour. Roll out Pizza Dough to ⅛-inch thick square and place on baking sheet.

In a sauté pan over medium heat, sauté shallots and mushrooms in 1 teaspoon extra-virgin olive oil with a pinch of salt and pepper until softened and lightly browned—about 8 minutes. Reserve in a bowl and wipe down the pan. Return the pan to the heat and add 2 tablespoons extra-virgin olive oil. Add sliced onions and sauté until dark and caramelized—about 15 minutes.

Arrange the mushroom-shallot mixture, caramelized onions, pine nuts, and cheeses on top of the dough. Bake until crispy and golden at edges—about 8 minutes. Remove from oven and let cool for about 30 seconds. Top with arugula and finish with Frantoio and a sprinkle of salt and pepper.

1 Ball Pizza Dough	1 Tablespoon toasted pine nuts
1 Tablespoon chopped shallots	2 Tablespoons grated Grana Padano cheese
¼ Cup chopped crimini mushrooms	4 Ounces Taleggio cheese
¼ Cup chopped chanterelle mushrooms	1 Handful arugula
3 Teaspoons extra-virgin olive oil	1 Tablespoon Frantoio olive oil
2 Tablespoons thinly sliced onions	Sea salt and black pepper

Pizza Dough
Makes one ten-ounce or two five-ounce individual pizza doughs

½ Cup warm water (105°F to 110°F)
1 ⅛ Teaspoon instant or rapid dry active yeast
½ Teaspoon sugar

¼ Teaspoon Kosher salt
1 Teaspoon extra-virgin olive oil, plus 2 teaspoons for proofing
1 ¼ Cups all-purpose flour, plus more for dusting

In a mixing bowl, combine flour, yeast, sugar, and salt. In a small glass or measuring cup, combine oil and warm water. Begin slowly pouring water mixture into bowl of dry ingredients, turning with a fork until a sticky ball of dough forms. Sift a little flour onto a table and pull dough from bowl to begin rolling. Add a dusting of flour while turning to form a smooth dough ball. Dough should be slightly tacky but not too sticky. If necessary, add more flour, 1 tablespoon at a time.

Add 2 teaspoons extra-virgin olive oil to a medium mixing bowl. Form dough into a ball and transfer to bowl, turning dough to coat with oil. Cover bowl with plastic and place in a warm, draft-free spot until doubled in size, about 45 minutes. Dough is ready to be rolled out or cut into 2 to make pizza.

Using a vegetable peeler, peel 1 large swath of peel (avoiding the white pith as much as possible) from the lemon and the grapefruit. Mince the peels and place in a small bowl. Cut the lemon and grapefruit in half, squeeze a few drops of juice from each over the peels, and add the Arbequina olive oil. Muddle the mixture (with a pestle, a muddler, or the back of a spoon) and set aside.

Preheat oven to 300°F. Season scallops on both sides with salt and pepper. In a sauté pan over medium-high heat, heat extra-virgin olive oil until it starts to smoke. Add scallops and sear on 1 side until nicely browned, about 2 minutes, then flip and cook the second side for 30 seconds more. Transfer scallops to a paper towel and let rest for 1 minute.

In the same hot pan, add baby kale and sauté until kale starts to wilt—about 20 to 30 seconds. Season with salt and pepper, remove from pan, and place kale in the center of each plate. Place ½ teaspoon 'Nduja atop each scallop, return to the warm pan, and place pan in oven until 'Nduja is warm—about 1 minute. Remove and set 2 scallops on each plate, alongside the baby kale. Spoon 1 to 2 teaspoons of lemon-grapefruit infused oil mixture over top, garnish each scallop with micro cilantro, and serve.

Day Boat Scallops have been harvested and brought in fresh from the first boat into the harbor.

Seared Day Boat Scallops
makes two servings

1 Small lemon
1 Small grapefruit
2 Tablespoons Arbequina olive oil
4 Large (U10) scallops
Salt and black pepper

2 Teaspoons extra-virgin olive oil
2 Cups packed baby kale
4 Sprigs micro cilantro
2 Teaspoons 'Nduja,* optional

available in specialty Italian markets

Shortbread Mascarpone with Amarena Cherries

Crème Brûlée

Chocolate Banana Bread Pudding

Chocolate Sponge Cake

Apple Tartine

Strawberry Crostata

DESSERTS

What do great films and meals at the commissary have in common? A memorable ending. You might just find yourself spooning bites of shortbread topped with luscious mascarpone and black cherries, slicing into warm apple tartine, cracking the just-torched surface of crème brûlée, or tucking into rich chocolate sponge cake. The folks at Warner Bros. aren't afraid to ask for seconds. We hope your experience is just as sweet.

Shortbread Mascarpone with Amarena Cherries

Preheat oven to 300°F. Line a baking sheet with parchment paper. Combine butter, cinnamon, and ½ cup sugar in a mixing bowl and use a stand or handheld mixer to beat until light and fluffy. Gradually mix in flour until well combined. Spread dough evenly across the parchment-lined baking sheet and bake until lightly browned—30 to 40 minutes. Remove from oven and immediately pierce all over with a fork; cut bars into 1-inch by 2-inch rectangles. (Note: This will yield approximately 16 cookies.) Cool cookies completely before removing from pan.

Combine mascarpone, Grand Marnier, lemon zest, vanilla, and remaining 2 tablespoons sugar in a mixing bowl; stir with a rubber spatula until well incorporated. Place in a covered container and refrigerate until chilled.

To assemble, take each cookie and spread 1 tablespoon of mascarpone mixture onto it. Top each cookie with 3 cherries and garnish with 1 sprig micro basil. Serve with cherry syrup (from the jar) drizzled around the perimeter of the plate.

makes four servings

1	Cup (2 sticks) salted butter, softened
½	Teaspoon cinnamon
½	Cup plus 2 tablespoons granulated sugar
2	Cups all-purpose flour
1	Cup soft mascarpone cheese
1	Ounce Grand Marnier
1	Teaspoon lemon zest
¼	Teaspoon vanilla extract
1	8-ounce jar Amarena cherries in syrup*
1	Package micro basil, for garnish

available in specialty marekts

Crème Brûlée

Preheat oven to 275°F. Split vanilla beans lengthwise and scrape out vanilla seeds with a knife or teaspoon. Place seeds and pods into a saucepan with cream and milk and slowly bring to a boil; as soon as the milk boils, remove from heat.

In a large bowl, use an electric mixer to beat egg yolks and sugar until light and fluffy. Remove vanilla pods from milk. Little by little, add hot milk to egg mixture, whisking continuously. Add a few inches of water to the (now-empty) saucepan and bring to a simmer. Place the bowl of custard on top of the pan (to form a double boiler) and cook, stirring often, until mixture thickens and coats the back of a spoon—about 5 minutes.

Divide custard mixture between 4 6-ounce ramekins (or cocottes). Stand ramekins in a high-sided roasting tray and fill tray with enough water to go halfway up ramekins. Place in oven and cook until mixture has set but is still slightly wobbly in the center—30 to 45 minutes. Cool at room temperature and place in refrigerator until ready.

To serve, sprinkle each custard with 1 tablespoon sugar and torch with a small blowtorch until a crisp, bruléed sugar shell forms. Garnish with berries, crème fraîche, and a mint leaf.

makes four servings

2	Vanilla beans
1¼	Cups heavy cream
¾	Cup plus 1 tablespoon low-fat milk
8	Large free-range egg yolks
⅓	Cup plus 4 tablespoons Granulated sugar
	Berries and mint leaves, for garnish
	Crème fraîche for garnish, optional

Chocolate Banana Bread Pudding

makes ten servings

4	Large eggs, lightly beaten
1	Cup milk
3	Cups heavy cream
1	Teaspoon pure vanilla extract
1	Cup light brown sugar
½	Teaspoon ground cinnamon
½	Teaspoon allspice
6	Cups ½-inch-diced, day-old brioche and croissants
8	Ounces bittersweet chocolate, chopped
3	Ripe bananas, mashed
3	Ounces Bulleit bourbon
6	Tablespoons unsalted butter, melted and cooled
	Confectioners' sugar and mint leaves, for garnish
2	Cups sweetened whipped cream, for serving

Preheat oven to 350°F. In a large mixing bowl, whisk eggs, milk, cream, vanilla, sugar, cinnamon, and allspice until sugar is dissolved. Stir in brioche and croissant cubes and let sit in the refrigerator for 1 hour, stirring occasionally. Stir in chocolate, bananas, and bourbon. Grease a 10-cup baking pan with the melted, cooled butter. Carefully pour in mixture and bake until pudding sets—about 1 to 1½ hours. Serve immediately, warm or at room temperature, garnished with confectioners' sugar and mint sprigs, with whipped cream on the side.

Chocolate Sponge Cake

makes two nine-inch cakes

2	Cups sugar
1¾	Cups all-purpose flour
¾	Cup Hershey's cocoa powder
1½	Teaspoons baking powder
1½	Teaspoons baking soda
1	Teaspoon salt
2	Eggs
1	Cup milk
½	Cup vegetable oil
2	Teaspoons vanilla extract
1	Cup boiling water

Preheat oven to 350°F. Grease and flour 2 9-inch round baking pans.

Stir together sugar, flour, cocoa, baking powder, baking soda, and salt in large mixing bowl. Add eggs, milk, oil, and vanilla. Beat with an electric mixer, on medium speed, for 2 minutes. Stir in boiling water (note: batter will be thin).

Pour batter into prepared pans. Bake 30 to 35 minutes, or until toothpick/cake tester inserted in center comes out clean. Cool 10 minutes, then remove from pans to wire racks. Cool completely before serving.

Apple Tartine

Preheat oven to 425°F. Coat a 10-inch ovenproof skillet with butter. Sprinkle sugar and cinnamon evenly over pan. Arrange apples in pan in a circular pattern, rounded sides down. Place skillet over medium-high heat and cook until sugar melts and begins to caramelize. Add cider and continue to cook until apples soften and caramel begins to brown—about 10 to 12 minutes. Remove from heat.

Sprinkle a work surface with flour and gently roll puff pastry dough into an 11-inch circle. Place crust over skillet and tuck edges around apples. Bake until crust is golden brown—about 20 minutes. Let cool for 5 minutes; then place a plate over the skillet and carefully invert to release the tart. (If any apples stick, just carefully scrape them off and place them back on top of crust.)

makes one ten-inch tart

4	**Tablespoons unsalted butter (preferably Plugra)**
¾	**Cup granulated sugar**
½	**Teaspoon cinnamon**
4	**Large Granny Smith apples, peeled, cored, and quartered**
¼	**Cup apple cider (preferably Martinelli's)**
1	**Tablespoon all-purpose flour**
1	**Sheet puff pastry, cut into a 10-inch circle**

Strawberry Crostata

Preheat oven to 350°F. In a small bowl, combine cinnamon with 1 tablespoon sugar. Remove phyllo from refrigerator and let soften until workable—about 15 minutes.

Gently peel off 5 sheets of phyllo at a time, brush each lightly with melted butter, and sprinkle with cinnamon-sugar mixture. Stack sheets on top of each other, overlapping and turning almost a quarter-turn per layer. The result should look like a star. Repeat with the remaining sheets, 5 sheets at a time; when finished, you should have 8 phyllo stars. Place stars atop cups of a large upside-down muffin tin so sides fall toward bottom. Place tin in oven and bake until crisp—about 12 to 15 minutes. Let cool before handling.

In a stainless steel mixing bowl, combine remaining 1 cup sugar, mascarpone, vanilla extract, and lemon zest. Mix with a rubber spatula until incorporated. In a separate bowl, combine strawberries and Grand Marnier and mix thoroughly.

To assemble, place a tiny dollop mascarpone mixture at center of plate and place a single phyllo shell atop. Fill shell with 7 tablespoons mascarpone mixture. Top with 4 tablespoons strawberry mixture, garnish with micro basil, drizzle Fig Balsamic Syrup around edge of plate, and serve.

makes eight servings

½	**Teaspoon cinnamon**
⅓	**Cup plus 1 tablespoon granulated sugar**
1	**1-pound box phyllo dough (40 sheets), defrosted and refrigerated (preferably Athens brand)**
¼	**Cup melted butter**
3	**Cups mascarpone cheese**
1	**Teaspoon vanilla extract**
	Zest from 1 lemon
2	**Cups strawberries, hulled and halved**
1	**Tablespoon Grand Marnier**
1	**Tablespoon micro basil leaves, for garnish**
1	**Teaspoon reduced Fig Balsamic Syrup**

(recipe on page 52)

Index

Photography Index

The first commissary, originally named The Green Room, which houses food service to this day.

A studio guest, Lauritz Melchoir, Jane Powell, Claude Jarman Jr., and Thomas E. Breen, circa 1948.

Inside the cafeteria.

A studio guest with Marie Wilson.

Jack L. Warner with Albert Einstein, who was visiting the studio, 1931.

Leon Schlesinger, producer Ben Kelmenson, and voice artist Mel Blanc, sitting at the Animation Department dinner party.

Actor Wayne Morris in costume.

Errol Flynn in his Adventures of Robin Hood costume, talking to Wayne Morris, 1938.

Frank Sinatra at a buffet spread outside his new bungalow (now building 102) on the Warner Lot, circa 1965.

Bette Davis and director William Wyler (middle, right) promoting The Letter, 1940.

Original First National Café menu, circa 1928.